IN THE NAME OF SANITY

IN
THE NAME
OF
SANITY

RAYMOND SWING

Harper & Brothers Publishers

NEW YORK · LONDON

Gratefully

to Mary

Table of Contents

Introduction

EARLY in the morning of August 24, 1945, I went for a long walk, in the course of which I came to a decision to announce that night in my regular broadcast that thereafter I should devote each Friday's talk to the influence of the release of atomic energy on our time. During the walk I saw certain problems clearly. The atomic bomb had changed warfare, and must change all social life. I recognized that I should have to discuss world government, since only through a world sovereignty could war be ablolished, and civilization preserved. It would not be easy for me to do this. As a news analyst I had never espoused any cause or doctrine in my broadcasts, as I believed that I did not have a right to do so. Now I should do so because I did not have the right not to. The atomic bomb blew up any good reasons I once might have had against taking such a course, I was driven by a large logic into a lesser inconsistency. I could rationalize the decision by saying that the atomic bomb was the most important news of the age, and that discussion of it was newsworthy. But I knew quite well I was changing the concept of my work, and that I really had no alternative. I did not, I trust, puff up my importance. I believe I know the limits of my day's work and influence. What I value primarily is the freedom to express myself without outside interference, which, to the credit of American radio—and my sponsors, I might say—I have been allowed and indeed encouraged to do. So I made my decision out of loyalty to my own vision of the truth. On that long, early-morning walk I saw that the human race was having a single chance to survive, and every member of it must do what he could to use the chance. I could answer for only one member, myself.

I did not, as did Norman Cousins in writing "Modern Man is Obsolete" for the *Saturday Review of Literature*, see my philosophy instantly and all of a piece. For Mr. Cousins poured forth the whole of that remarkable editorial on the night of the news of the bombing of Hiroshima. For my part, though I had known that some of our greatest scientists were working for the government under a heavy cloak of secrecy, I had not deduced that they were engaged on the release of atomic energy. And the news of the bombing of Hiroshima surprised me. But like all other lay readers of science I was prepared for the release of atomic energy. Probably I was even too ingenuous in believing it was bound to come and might well come in my day. As one who had not been able to pass Freshman mathematics I am well below par in intelligence in these matters. I had been utterly baffled by Professor Bohr's quantum theory. And when I was told that the atom is a little solar system in which the minute planets, instead of circling decorously in their orbits, jerk about without rhyme or reason, I confess to having had my doubts. Still, when the news came of Hiroshima I was able to grasp that an era had ended and an era had begun. I was not frightened at first. Beyond justification, as I later found, I felt elated over a new freedom now in wait for mankind. The scientists were soon to impress it on us all that the peacetime use of atomic energy is still years away, and that it will be a limited use when it comes. The greater scope may well be justified later on, but it cannot be predicted with certainty, and definitely not with a timetable. The release of atomic energy, as Dr. Einstein was to assure us, is for the present a menace and only a menace. So I had to learn to be frightened, rather than to take the more usual course of learning not to be.

I was on vacation when news of Hiroshima was announced. I listened to many discussions of the bomb on the air and thought that if I were to talk about it I should be much more extreme in my statements. Domestically I was sure it meant socialism, since no people could allow such great resources of power to be governed by individual or corporation. Internationally I was sure it meant world government, for that would be the only way to abolish war, which had to be abolished if civilization were to endure. That was as far as my own thinking took me at the time. And then I realized day after day that the world had changed, that the old order which I had left in going for my brief holiday had vanished by the time I had returned. So I took my walk and came to my decision, to devote four of each week's broadcasts to the obsolete world, and only one to the real one. Even that was a timid partition of time.

The broadcasts are a kind of crude chart of the thinking in the weeks following the announcement of the atomic bomb. They show the rise of hope in President Truman as a conscious and courageous leader toward world government, and then the chilling realization that he had not chosen this destiny or endeavored to rise to it. The broadcasts surpassed my expectations as conveyances of news. I was able to give the first comprehensive account of Dr. Einstein's letter and Dr. Szilard's memorandum which Alexander Sachs took to President Roosevelt in 1939, which was the genesis of the atomic bomb project. I was able to publish the first resolution of the Oak Ridge scientists, and so have a little part in the remarkable introduction of the atomic scientists to their countrymen. Dr. Einstein's first pronouncement on the atomic bomb could be made through one of these talks. And the May-Johnson bill there received one of its first public criticisms.

As to the Oak Ridge scientists, and indeed all the atomic scientists, a word should be said to counter the impression among some that these men are naïve or inexperienced in public affairs. They speak differently from the politicians, and come to different conclusions. They are more simple and direct. But what is not sufficiently appreciated is that the atomic scientists are two or more years ahead of us in thinking about the significance of atomic energy. And that is what accounts for their simple, direct conclusions. When summoned under conditions of romantic secrecy to work on the atomic bomb project, they had their first inkling of what they were doing. They had not worked long before they could see that probably they were going to succeed. And thereafter these men were steeped in thought about the social implications of what they were doing. They were away from home, thrown in upon each other, and so living in conditions permitting them to think and discuss without much interruption. They began their thinking socially with a head start on the rest of us, because they did not need to be instructed about atomic energy, or the force or the danger of it.

The conclusions they reached by the time they made their entry upon the national stage were the conclusions you and I are likely to reach by the time we have done as much thinking as they have done. We may mistakenly believe that the scientists are ingenuous and inexperienced, when the fact is that it is we who are ingenuous and inexperienced, the politicians as well as the rest of us. At present the scientists know more about the political problem of atomic energy than the politicians, not because they are better politicians, but because the politicians have just begun to do any thinking whatever about the world as changed by atomic energy. When they have thought about it awhile, no doubt they will become wiser politicians than the scientists. But for the present the scientists are way ahead of them in their own field. If we want a preview of what we are likely to be thinking in two years, we can have it in what the scientists are now saying. While it is true that the scientist is no better fitted to discuss politics than any other craftsman, it also is true that the conclusions he reaches are most probably the same that anyone else with intelligence will come to, given an understanding of the problem. The scientist starts with an understanding of the problem, which is his only advantage. And we shall all reach the same general destination. We shall see that the weapons of war have now reached a power which can destroy us, so that if we wish not to be destroyed we must end the use of the weapons. And since the weapons cannot be effectively banned if war is to continue, there is no choice but to end war.

The same syllogism can be stated in terms of law. For war is anarchy in the relationship of nations. And the only way to have peace is to extend the reign of law to international relations, and to organize a power that will enact law and enforce it. We are familiar with the syllogism when stated in terms of law, and we might well have applied ourselves to the creation of world law in a few generations. More of the common people of America believe in world government than the sophisticated may realize. A resolution memorializing Congress to take the initiative for the establishment of world federal government has passed thirteen state legislatures in this country, and the theme has reached the ears of men and women in hamlet and village with more force than it has the drawing-rooms of the cities of the eastern seaboard. The name of Robert Lee Humber is not known to Park Avenue and Massachusetts Avenue, but it is known the length and breadth of many Main Streets. Dr. Oppenheimer and his earnest colleagues have taken away the time in which the Robert Lee Humbers were going to operate. Instead of in a few generations, the same work must be done at once. And the function of the scientists is to make us know that we must move with a celerity never before shown by human beings. Having blown us out of our lethargy, they come inescapably to the same conclusion as those who think about peace in the language of law. For there can be no other peace in a world of power. At best there can be a truce, long or short, as the case may be. And in a world of atomic energy, the truce is worthless save as an interim in which to establish world law. Otherwise it is simply a prelude to destruction.

We are confronted by a first danger, the destructiveness of applied atomic energy. And then we are confronted by a second danger, that we do not enough appreciate the first danger. Only a short time has passed since the bomb was perfected. Already it seems to have shrunk to something smaller in its awful dimensions—not in fact, for in fact a bomb much more powerful than the one used on Nagasaki is available—but through the corrosion of familiarity. We were frightened for a time and then surmounted our fears, doing so in an incredibly stupid way. Our fears have not led us yet to take the lead nationally to abolish war, so our danger is precisely as great as it was last August. Indeed I should say that it is considerably greater, because our original policy in keeping the bomb a secret made the building of wholesome relations with the Soviet Union far more difficult. We surmounted our fears by the time-honored human way of denying them. Like the man in the fable who knew that if he lived through March he would live the rest of the year *because he always had*, we have begun to feel safe because we are able to feel at all. We go on recklessly subscribing to national and international policies, and tolerating dinner-table and fireside conversations which bring war appreciably nearer. And though we ought to know that collisions in politics occur in answer to a kind of law of magnetism, we blame the Russians, as the Russians blame us, for being drawn into a conflict. We do nothing to de-electrify the magnetism which draws us together, in fact we deliriously find a kind of safety in not being already destroyed by our folly. We seem to think there is no potency in lightning because it has not yet struck us down for not believing in it.

So a great problem during the months ahead is to overcome lethargy. We are like a man lost in a blizzard who is combating the numbness of his limbs and the furtive thoughts that tell him he might as well succumb and stop striving to keep going. If we do not press on, against every temptation to relax, we shall be overpowered. The release of atomic energy is not a novelty which loses its potency if we only stop thinking about it. Modern man was as obsolete on August 13, 1945, as Norman Cousins said he was. Today he is even more obsolete. Many months have passed and he still does not have world government. He still lives in a system of nations which permits war. I am not saying these things can happen in a few months. Obviously years are needed to achieve them. I am only saying that the time grows shorter every moment, and until we are safe we are in danger. But I also am saying we are less safe than we were on August 13, 1945, and our danger increases steadily from now on.

We have one biological comfort, that life often finds ways of contriving conduct permitting its own survival. It will satisfy

this biological need if the people of America, understanding their
danger and the practicability of living safely, will think through
the problems of the bomb, and the problems of anarchy and law
in international relations. Once we have sincerely concluded
that we do not want sovereignty for war-making purposes, we
shall have made a new world as surely as the atomic bomb has
made it, or rather, only in this way can the atomic bomb make a
new world. When we, as a nation, renounce sovereignty for war-
making purposes, we remove fear from our relations with other
nations. Without fear of us they will cease to behave according
to the promptings of fear. They can begin to relax some of the
internal rigors they have adopted because of their fear. They
can channel their expenditure of energy and manpower to the
activities of peace, rather than the demands of defense. By
removing their fear, we shall have made place for their confidence. Like fear, confidence is magnetic, so that we too shall
become less afraid. I have every confidence that the American
people will understand how to make use of the magnetic power
of peace, once they have thought about it.

CHAPTER I

"One World or No World"

WITHOUT promising to be rigid about it, I intend to devote all or nearly all of every Friday broadcast for some time to the world as made new by the release of atomic energy. I am doing this, in the first place, to meet my sense of news values. All the rest of the week I shall deal with the current problems of this country and the world, which you and I know are out of date. They demonstrate that modern man is obsolete, as the *Saturday Review of Literature* puts it. My proportions would be nearer right if I talked about an atomic world four nights and about the doings of the old and obsolete world for only one night while it dawdles off the stage.

The view has already been expressed that since others will learn the secret of making the atomic bomb in four or five years, there is no point in keeping it a secret. But it must be controlled by a world government. And we have only four or five years in which to start creating this world government, if it is to be ready in time to guarantee that the world will not be destroyed. World government appears to me to be the greatest political need that ever pressed on the human race. It is the most urgent social necessity that you or I or any of our ancestors have ever been asked to face, so there are bound to be intensely dramatic developments. Louis Adamic wrote to me his idea of a key phrase for this time. It is "One world or no world." That sums up the situation as it is. There must be one world, or the many worlds into which we still are divided by our archaic concepts of sovereignty will wipe each other out. I might say that even without atomic energy, one world was a requisite because of the assured future of rocket bombs capable of flight to any part of the world under electronic control. But we had more time to unify to save ourselves from these weapons. Now we have four or five years in which to lay an entirely new foundation of international government. And that means five years in which to make over, first of all, our minds.

In the British parliament, on August 23, 1945, the charter of the United Nations was ratified without a dissenting vote. But there was a great deal of dissent. The debate was really about the atomic bomb and its control. It was realized that it is necessary to insure control of atomic energy, and that if this is done there will be world peace. If not, the United Nations charter means little. That is how Herbert Matthews summed up the debate for the New York *Times*. The question was frankly asked of Secretary Bevin why the Soviet Union should not be given the secret of the atomic bomb. He answered with a question: "To whom are we to give the secret? Merely to the three or the five of the world organization? I think," he went on, "we must postpone consideration of this until the world organization is established, and we see clearly how matters stand. The whole question of dangerous weapons is one that we must discuss together. Dangerous weapons cannot be made without essential raw materials and we have to see that these essential materials are as much controlled as the finished product. The peace of the world depends on the unanimity of the great powers. There must always be differences between them on many subjects, but there must be a united decision as to the necessity of avoiding such differences as would lead to war."

This reply of the foreign secretary of one of the first three governments of the world shows how much stumbling and fumbling there is in high places. For the peace of the world cannot depend on the unanimity of the great powers if some of the great powers have a secret weapon of fearful capacity not possessed by another great power and deliberately kept from that power. This was sensed in the House of Commons. Mr. Zilliacus, a Labor member who for years was on the staff of the League of Nations, said that he hoped the council of Ministers

—the Foreign Ministers of the Big Five—would "make it perfectly clear that they do not propose to play Anglo-American atomic power politics against the Soviet Union." That remark should bring all of us in this country up short. The wide public here certainly will not permit power politics to be played by the United States against anybody, and first of all not against the Soviet Union, since that surely would lead to war. And it can be said with certainty that the Truman administration has no thought of playing power politics against the Soviet Union. One may have doubts when the military and navy people get to talking about bases in the Pacific. For there is no secret about it that these are conceived of as needed for security, and the security is against someone, and that someone, in addition to Japan, is the Soviet Union. But even the military and naval people are thinking in terms of security against, not the power to attack. But that distinction, while it may be utterly valid so far as we are concerned, is not valid once the problem is looked at with other eyes than our own. And our determination to keep the secret of the atomic bomb to ourselves looks far different to a Russian from the way it does to us. We know that we want no conquest, we do not seek to dominate others, we are a peaceful nation which aspires to see the establishment of a regime of law throughout the world, based upon the freedom, justice and the dignity of man. But others do not appraise us as we appraise ourselves. Have you ever stopped to think what we should feel if the Russians possessed the atomic bomb and had not offered the secret to us? We should be frightened. To a certain extent we should know we were put at the mercy of the Soviet Union, a country which has different, and we think inferior, values from ours in matters of government. We should be certain that the Soviet Union had not offered the secret to us for the very reason that it wished us to be at its mercy to a certain extent. That, you may be sure, is what the Russians think of us. They read the anti-Russian press in this country; I am sure they attach far too much importance to it; they are convinced that the dominant people in this country regard the atomic bomb as giving us power over all others, and in the first place over themselves. They suspect that we are basically un-friendly and potentially hostile to them. So they feel insecure. And for the moment, instead of the peace bringing us into an era with freedom from fear, we ourselves have created fear, and our policy, if it continues on the same line, will create more fear. And out of fear grows war. In fear is the danger of war. And we have not started off in this atomic age as a benign leader of the human race. We are failing to be benign not out of intent, but out of unfamiliarity with the problem. We are stumbling and fumbling just as much as Mr. Bevin, only it is more serious for us to stumble and fumble because we have the bomb, and the leadership of the world.

Senator Downey of California knows this. On August 24, 1945, he urged Congress to give "serious consideration" to the possibility of making the secret of atomic power available to the world through the United Nations Organization. And he also warned that unless America develops the industrial use of atomic power to the full we run the risk of becoming a third-rate power within fifteen or twenty years. Senator Downey was not too sure himself. He said he is not ready yet to advocate disclosure of the secret to the world. All he thought was that the possibility should be seriously considered. As to Russia, he said, "You can imagine the suspicion and bitterness we would feel if we didn't have it and Russia did. Our whole aim would be to outdo Russia in a race for bigger and better atomic bombs."

To this I should like to add that release of the atomic secret through the United Nations would be going only a little way toward solving the problem of atomic power. It has to be con-trolled. For in time the very irresponsible may obtain bombs and may be able to destroy the rest of us. So much power can-not be left to sovereign states. There can be only one sovereign, the world itself. And it must have command and control of the manufacture of atomic bombs, far more rigidly than any sovereign state ever commanded and controlled the weapons which could lead to its own internal downfall. It will be impos-sible to control without inspection answerable to a central federal power. Inspection requires the existence of a super-sovereignty.

Sir George Paget Thomson, chairman of the British committee set up to study the wartime development of atomic power, holds out a doubtful hope and comfort for those who are not ready for world government. Future wars, he declared, will be no worse than past ones. In World War II the weapons were more formidable than those of the last war, but he points out that British losses in men were only a third as great; and Germany's losses were fewer than in the Thirty Years War, when gunpowder was in its infancy. "If there is another war and atomic bombs are used, I don't believe the number of people killed," he said, "will be greater than in this war and might well be less, since it is easier to protect people than machinery from violent explosion because it is easier to disperse them. The objectives will be factories, not armies. Towns will be evacuated when relations between countries become strained, and atomic bombs are too valuable to be wasted on the countryside." But Hiroshima is a measure of the comfort to be had from what Sir George Thomson says. The dead there numbered thirty thousand in the first days after the explosion, then rose to sixty thousand. And the Japanese say the radio-activity engendered in the region continued to destroy people for weeks afterward. They seemed to be well, then they succumbed to mysterious injury as though eaten by penetrating rays. The count of both white and red corpuscles went way down below the danger mark. And as for the city, ninety per cent of it was destroyed by the first explosion. If there are to be factories, as Sir George admits, then the death toll will be shockingly high, if Hiroshima is an index.

Obviously, we can move our cities underground. That is the surest defense against the rocket-bomb, and one assumes it will be a sure defense against the atomic bomb, though its capacities have not been fully developed. But if that is to be done, it must be started at once. "Either world government, or a world underground," is another way to describe the choice before us. If we are not going to use the next five years to get started on creating world government, we must build cities underground at unheard of speed to have them ready in time.

CHAPTER II

Sovereignty Must Be Limited

WE CANNOT bomb our way into physical security or moral unity." This statement sums up what leading scholars of science, philosophy and religion, who met in their annual conference in New York during the last week in August, think about the atomic bomb. They found that atomic power, like all other forms of power, is an opportunity as well as a peril. And they declared that "it is more clear than ever that we can, if we will, create a world of greater happiness, knowledge, and breadth of moral and spiritual outlook; or failing that, we shall discover that we have loosed energies which will imperil civilization as we know it."

These men issued a grave warning to this country. "America, above all," they said, "must in these days be careful not to be dazzled with the prospect of world power which has come to her. America's greatness is the result of the moral leadership she offered mankind in the early days of her existence, the days of Washington, Jefferson, Madison and Lincoln."

They complain that many in present-day America are blind to moral and spiritual values, as witnessed by their unwillingness to make the feeding of the hungry in Europe and Asia, and the reconstruction of their economy, a major responsibility of the American people. "To believe," they said, "that it is to the interest of our children in the last analysis to be well fed while the rest of the world starves, is both wicked and foolish. To hope for a peaceful world which will be permanently dependent on us, economically and militarily, is to hope for that which cannot be, because it should not be."

When it came to positive proposals, however, the conference let it go with a recommendation of re-education from aggressiveness to co-operative, peaceful endeavors.

Sir John Anderson, Chancellor of the Exchequer in the Churchill government, and appointed by Mr. Churchill to be responsible for atomic research, probably knows more about the four years of work that produced the atomic bomb than any other man in England. He is not content to wait for re-education. "These are problems," he said, "calling for statesmanship of the highest order. The establishment of any organization for the maintenance of world peace and security would obviously be sheer mockery if means cannot be found of guaranteeing the effective control of an instrument of war of such potency. There could be no higher task for the statesmen of the United Nations gathered around the conference table."

The effective control of the atomic bomb is what the scholars of philosophy, science and religion would agree, I am sure, is a start on re-education to co-operative endeavors. It would be the exercise of moral and spiritual force, which they urged.

In my first broadcast on the atomic bomb, I spoke of world government as the greatest political need that ever pressed on the human race. I had an interesting rejoinder from one listener. He is a bishop, who wrote me that we have just put world security in the hands of a World Security Council, and if that body controls the use of the atomic bomb that is all that is needed. He closed with a piece of advice. "Don't be a prophet," his letter ended. "It is easy to become a fool."

Maybe I should have explained that in saying we have only a few years to get started on world government I had no thought that world government can be achieved fully in that time. It will come but much more slowly. I was thinking of a limited government, dealing only with those matters which cannot be left to the individual states without danger that they will destroy each other and civilization. It would be a world government vested with the power to control the making of atomic bombs and rocket bombs. That is how it must start. From there it can grow into something more—and I think that it will—and so bring only more and more happiness and solidarity to the human family. But it cannot be launched for these ultimate aims and achieved soon, since lasting social institutions have to grow slowly. But in a great emergency, when states or civilization are in peril, emergency action must be taken.

But I disagree with the bishop that all that is needed is to let the World Security Council control the use of the atomic bomb. That could mean that the World Security Council would be the only authority with a right to say when the bomb should be used, or it could mean that it should be the only authority with the right to make as well as use the bomb. To be the only one with authority to use the bomb is no guarantee that somebody without authority will not use it. So that is no security. And if the World Security Council is the only authority to make as well as to use the bomb, then it is something much, much more than the existing World Security Council. It is what I advocated, the beginning of world government. For to be the only one to make the bomb requires power. The Supreme Security Council would have to be the only sovereign in this domain, and would have to clip the sovereignty of all otherwise sovereign states. And that would be super-sovereignty and the start of world government.

Before we reach that point, however, several important steps need to be taken. The President himself, when he told the public about the atomic bomb, said that normally the government and our own scientists would not withhold knowledge from the world. But he said that under present circumstances it was not intended to divulge the technical processes or all the military applications, pending further examination of possible methods of protecting us and the rest of the world from the danger of sudden destruction.

He said he would recommend that Congress consider the establishment of an appropriate commission to control the production and use of atomic power within the United States. And he would make further recommendations to Congress as to how atomic power can become a powerful and forceful influence toward the maintenance of world peace. Use of atomic power within the United States means use for industrial and medical purposes. That is to be controlled by the government. And if atomic energy is to be the source of any great part of our domestic power, that walks us right into at least part-way socialism.

But the use of the atomic bomb toward the maintenance of world peace is not something we can do alone. There will be many persons with lusty voices, who will argue that we can and that we should do it alone. They are a new brand of inverted isolationists, who quite foolishly believe that we can keep the atomic bomb a permanent secret and that the world peace should be only a Pax Americana. But we cannot keep it a permanent secret. And the moment any other state has it and so chooses that is the end of any Pax Americana. It not only would be poor morals for us to try to be the most powerful nation telling all nations how to live under our dispensation, it also is not practicable. And these inverted isolationists, like the prewar variety, have their ostrich heads in the same old sand.

I wish to recommend two major steps to be taken to put us into a proper relation with the world about the atomic bomb, and into a proper relation with our own consciences. We should announce that we will not use the atomic bomb against any country except under instructions of the World Security Council. The British and Canadians should join us in a similar announcement. That would reassure the world that we are not going to play American power politics, or Anglo-Saxon power politics, with the atomic bomb. That would clear up the relationship with the world until a start can be made on building anew the world security organization.

And then we should take the most important step of modern times. We should announce that the release of atomic energy has made it impossible to maintain unlimited sovereignty for nations and that we are prepared to take the leadership and responsibility to initiate the earliest consultation on rebuilding the United Nations Organization. We must seek to give it powers not only to use the atomic bomb exclusively but to have the monopoly of its manufacture, along with the manufacture of the V-bombs and weapons of similarly destructive force.

I would not advocate turning over the secret of the atomic bomb to other nations until this new organization is completed. But I would have the United States demonstrate its good faith, its unselfishness and its moral and spiritual responsibility by pledging that this new organization will be begun, and that the secret of the atomic bomb will be turned over to it. If we, now the most powerful nation economically, and with our huge naval, air and army establishment by far the most powerful nation militarily, and with the atomic bomb uniquely strong as compared with any other power in history, thus offer to curtail our own sovereignty, we shall have lived up to the moral precedents of our great spiritual leaders, Washington, Jefferson, Madison and Lincoln. We shall have proved ourselves worthy of having developed atomic energy, we shall have demonstrated ourselves to be earnest custodians of civilization and true disciples of peace.

Here is a program I am sure a vast majority of Americans would subscribe to, and one must hope that when Congress has to act on the future of the atomic bomb it will sense the profound desire of the American people for an approach on this level.

Senator Vandenberg has declared that the control of the atomic bomb by the Security Council can be only after it has "the absolutely free and untrammeled rights of intimate inspection all around the globe." And he added, "Unfortunately that is a freedom that does not exist today." I am not sure that Senator Vandenberg meant to dismiss the idea, as has been presumed. His analysis is altogether right. If the bomb is to be controlled by the Council there has to be free and intimate inspection. And free and intimate inspection means curtailment of sovereignty. Senator Vandenberg has been a spokesman for unlimited sovereignty. But that does not mean that he now values sovereignty above civilization. Mr. Vandenberg has proved himself capable of growth and leadership. He may well see, and have the courage to proclaim, that the atomic bomb has made unlimited sovereignty obsolete. Even if he does not, the American people as a whole can be expected to see it, and so to order their affairs.

CHAPTER III

History of the Bomb

IN BERLIN, back in the early 1920's, I came upon something I thought the most irrational conduct I could well imagine. It was a mass meeting, held in the hall of the Philharmonic, to protest against the theory of relativity of Dr. Albert Einstein. The meeting was crowded, and, as I recall it, was addressed by at least one fairly reputable scientist. The purpose of the meeting, of course, was anti-Semitic, and the intention was to disparage the scientific work which had already won world-wide notice and acclaim for Dr. Einstein. I simply could not understand how anyone in his right mind hoped to prove that the theory of relativity was wrong by declaiming against it in a mass meeting.

As early as 1905, Dr. Einstein clearly stated that mass and energy are equivalent. He also stated that this equivalence might be found by the study of radio-active substances. He set down his formula, E equals mc^2, perhaps the most startling and far-reaching assertion of its kind ever made. For it says that energy is the equivalent of mass, multiplied by the square of the speed of light. To put this statement into numbers, and quoting the Smyth report, one kilogram of matter—just over two pounds —if converted into energy, would give 25,000,000,000 kilowatt hours of energy, or as much as is generated in nearly two months by the entire electric power equipment of the United States. So scientists have been familiar with this concept for a long time. Some of them accepted it as probably true, but undemonstrable. Some dared to believe that one day atomic energy would be unlocked and give man the use of power beyond his most fantastic dreams, since he then could wield the basic power of the universe itself.

I am not going into the history of the development of atomic research. I do wish it could be made simple and could be grasped by everyone. For unless the mind fathoms at least a little of the depths of meaning of man using atomic power, there can be no wise political action which makes that use safe and beneficial.

But I am going to tell a little of the history of the development of the atomic bomb which has not been more than referred to in the government release on the project.

It brings me once more to the name of Dr. Einstein. The mass meeting in the Philharmonic in Berlin had not affected the theory of relativity, but the organized bigotry behind it had led the great physicist and mathematician to go abroad, and finally to take up his home at Princeton. And there, on August 2, 1939, just a month before the outbreak of World War II, he wrote a remarkable letter. It is not as remarkable as that formula that E equals mc². But it is the letter that appropriately led to the development of the atomic bomb, and the demonstration of the validity of the formula. So it was a step to the expansion into another dimension of the power available to the human race.

This letter was addressed to "F. D. Roosevelt, President of the United States, White House, Washington." It starts with the sentence: "Some recent work by E. Fermi and L. Szilard, which has been communicated to me in manuscript, leads me to expect that the element uranium may be turned into a new and important source of energy in the immediate future."

It happens that this letter did not reach President Roosevelt until after the outbreak of war. It was not posted to him. It was taken to him, along with scientific memoranda and data, by Alexander Sachs of New York City. Mr. Sachs is one of the most brilliant of living economists. He is also a noted student of world affairs, and one of the most brilliant analysts of them. And he is a friend of Dr. Einstein. Both he and Dr. Einstein

believed in August 1939 that catastrophe hung over the human
race, and that in the course of that catastrophe atomic energy
would have a part. They felt they must bring the latest news
of atomic research to the knowledge of the President in the
cause of national defense.

Let me quote another passage from Dr. Einstein's letter to
President Roosevelt. "In the course of the last four months it
has been made probable," he stated, "through the work of Joliot
in France, as well as Fermi and Szilard in America, that it
may become possible to set up a nuclear chain reaction in a
large mass of uranium, by which vast amounts of power and
large quantities of new radium-like elements would be generated.
Now it appears almost certain that this would be achieved in
the immediate future." Dr. Einstein went on: "This new phe-
nomenon would also lead to the construction of bombs, and it
is conceivable—though much less certain—that extremely powerful bombs of a new type may thus be constructed. A single
bomb of this type, carried by boat and exploded in a port, might
very well destroy the whole port, together with some of the
surrounding territory. However, such bombs might very well
prove to be too heavy for transportation by air."

This was a few months after Hitler had seized Prague, and
Dr. Einstein told the President that Hitler thereupon had
stopped the sale of uranium from the Czechoslovakian mines.
This action, he suggested, was linked with the fact that the
son of the German Secretary of State von Weizaecker was
attached to the Kaiser Wilhelm Institute in Berlin, where some
of the American work on uranium was at that time being
repeated. Dr. Einstein recommended that the President appoint
someone on his behalf to keep government departments informed
of developments, who could also give attention to obtaining
a supply of uranium for the United States, and that experi-
mental work in this country be speeded up.

With the material Mr. Sachs took to President Roosevelt
on October 11, 1939, was a memorandum by the physicist
Szilard, one of the men whose work at Columbia had brought

uranium research to the brink of culmination. His statement reported that investigations so far had been limited to chain reactions based on the action of slow neutrons. "At present," he said, "it is an open question whether such a chain reaction can also be made to work with the fast neutrons which are not slowed down. There is reason to believe," he continued, "that if fast neutrons could be used, it would be easy to construct extremely dangerous bombs. The destructive power of these bombs can only be roughly estimated, but there is no doubt that it would go far beyond all military conceptions." I hardly need to interpolate that the fast reactions were made to work, which is the secret of the atomic bomb as it was finally used.

To his everlasting credit, President Roosevelt grasped fully what he was told, instructed his aide, General Watson, to act as liaison in the matter, and asked Dr. Lyman Briggs of the Bureau of Standards to constitute a committee of the armed services, a committee on which Mr. Sachs served as representing the President.

There were tedious delays before the atomic project was to be turned over to the entirely new National Research Committee under Dr. Vannevar Bush, which brought the bomb to reality. Of the several physicists consulted, some were anything but sanguine of success. Dr. Einstein and Professor Szilard were the ones most outspokenly confident that results could be achieved. A preliminary experiment at Columbia had to be waited for. It was on a small scale, but it turned out astonishingly favorably, so the Briggs Committee was able to recommend further action. But, in the meantime, priceless months were dribbling away, and the Germans were working on uranium with all scientists available to them.

Our Navy Department put up $6,000 to buy some materials. And another memorandum about atomic power by Professor Szilard spoke of the possibility of driving battleships with atomic engines. If only slow neutrons were utilized, a ton of uranium, he said, would equal 3,000 tons of oil; if the fast neutrons could be utilized, one ton of uranium would equal

300,000 tons of oil. A battleship with such a reserve of energy could stay away from fuel resources almost indefinitely.

On March 7, 1940, Dr. Einstein felt the need for greater haste. This was during the "Phony War" period, with the invasion of the western democracies imminent. "Since the outbreak of the war," he wrote, "interest in uranium has intensified in Germany. I have now learned that research there is being carried out in great secrecy and that it has been extended to another of the Kaiser Wilhelm institutes, the Institute of Physics." Dr. Einstein spoke of the need to keep scientists in the democracies from publishing their work on setting up a chain reaction in uranium. Dr. Szilard himself had written up a method for setting up the chain reaction. Later the effort was made to have the physicists in the democracies withhold their work from publication, so as to keep news of it from the Germans. The British agreed, but because one manuscript already had been inadvertently published, the French balked. Later, of course, this research became the top secret of all top secrets.

The war itself was to bring pressure on the project at this stage. By April 27, after the invasion of Norway, the Briggs Committee was ready to recommend further action, as the doubtful Thomases among its members became much less doubtful. On May 10, the very day of the German invasion of Holland, Belgium and France, the four chief Columbia University scientists, Fermi, Szilard, Pegram and Urey, were ready to plump for a large-scale experiment, that would cost anything up to half a million dollars.

And so it became clear that a bigger and better functioning organization was needed to take the place of the modest Briggs Committee. Mr. Sachs recommended his views to the President, and that was the genesis of the National Research Defense Committee under Vannevar Bush, which handled the $2,000,-000,000 and produced the atomic bomb. Naturally what this committee accomplished is the main part of the story. But before this could be done there had to be a chain of actions, which in the field of government can be as difficult to assure as in treating the atoms of uranium. Genius, friendship and patriotism, and in the President, the intelligence to know what it all could mean, had to combine to get the most original of all government projects under way.

To come back to that anti-Einstein mass meeting in Berlin, indirectly it served this country, fabulously, as did the tyranny in Germany and Italy, in bringing us the services of great scientists whose joint efforts produced the release of atomic energy.

CHAPTER IV

Living Dangerously

I HAVE told the story of the foresight which led to the United States government's getting started on building the atomic bomb in time to finish it before the end of the war. The foresight of comparatively few persons was necessary, for it was to be an enterprise of phenomenal secrecy.

Now that the atomic bomb has been made, now that it has burst, now that we know the terrestrial power of it, there must again be foresight, this time not of a few but of citizens of all the world. During the war the objective of the foresight was destruction. Today the objective is to save much of the human race from destruction. To destroy needed only an assignment to scientists and engineers financed by funds for which no accounting had to be made while they were being spent. To avert destruction requires political action, which has to be based on knowledge and ethics.

During the week of September 14 the Gallup poll turned up with an answer to the question whether the United States should keep the secret of the atomic bomb. To this seventy-three per cent answered yes. But the question really misses the point, since it presupposes that the United States *can* keep the secret. Assuming that it can, it is only natural that the nation having overwhelming power as against other nations, and convinced of its own righteousness, will vote to keep the power. It is simply a way of saying, let us remain overwhelmingly powerful. I don't grant it is a wise answer even then, but it is a very human one. However, it is not a factual answer. It has to do only with a world of wishes, not with a world of modern physics.

The atomic bomb cannot be kept a secret, and the problem is what to do about it for the very brief time in which our exclusive possession of it is a means of persuasion. Research in nuclear physics, which produced the atomic bomb, is the joint product of the men of many nations. A Russian is credited with having been among the first to achieve the essential chain reaction. Even the Japanese have already made plutonium. The secret of the bomb is more in the domain of engineering than of physical theory. And the physicists in other lands will have good engineers to advise them.

So there is no question about our keeping or sharing the secret. We shall have to share it whether we like it or not. The question is whether to share it now. It would put a terrible weapon in the hands of any government which has yet to demonstrate its trustworthiness. And in saying this I am thinking of no government in particular. But surely any government with Fascist tendencies, hence with warlike tendencies, should not be given the bomb, that to start with. But to go on from there, the question is whether any sovereign state whatever should be permitted to have the bomb, our own country included.

Here I suggest that one must ask: Are there to be wars in the future which might involve this country? The answer to that is yes, for as the United Nations Charter is written, wars between nations are possible, and we are sure to be involved in any great war. If there are wars in which our enemies have the atomic bomb, and we have it, the wars promise to be so destructive as to destroy civilization, ours and theirs. Add to the atomic bomb the guided missiles developed by the Germans, and future wars become so catastrophic that they cease to have political meaning.

Until now wars always *could* be won. At any rate, they decided the national destinies one way or the other for winner and loser. But future wars will be wholly lost by both sides. Furthermore, future wars will not be waged soldier versus soldier, but scientist and engineer versus civilian. Indeed, military wars appear to be over. All wars are to be against man, woman and child in their homes or their places of work.

So the problem is bigger than the atomic bomb and the guided missile, it is the problem of not having wars. The atomic bomb and the controlled missile have put an end to the practicability of war. We must so organize society that wars between nations are impossible. If we have wars, it is almost inevitable that the new weapons will be used. If we try simply to control the use of the weapons, and do not abolish wars, we shall be deluding ourselves.

So long as there are sovereign states with military power which they can use against each other, we live perpetually on the threshold of war. So what we need to do is to place all military power in the possession of a union of nations which will exercise all of that military power, and leave none of it to sovereign states. Then there will be no national wars. Then, at worst, there will be police action, either small action, or if some nation tries to secede, big action. But it will not be war for political ends. It will be the police action which enforces the law. In such a conflict, since it will be police action, civilization will be saved and strengthened, not destroyed. The terrible weapons need not be used. Man, woman and child again will be safe in their homes and their places of work.

I notice, among others, two streams of thinking among those I have heard discuss these problems. One stream approaches the problem in terms of controlling the new weapons, which entails inspection, and which, to mean anything, will have to be international inspection. The other stream starts off frankly with the concept of world government—a limited government at the outset, dealing perhaps only with security, but broadening as the years pass to include further federal activities. Both these streams reach the same ocean, for both recognize that the ultimate objective is world government. Both types are useful. But the man who prefers to think of control and inspection is likely to be the kind of man who takes first steps first, without being too sure of the steps to follow; while the man who plumps right off for world government may be inclined to be impatient with the man who concentrates on the next step.

I also meet those who think it would be enough to leave the atomic bomb with the Security Council of the United Nations as now constituted. And I know some of the seventy-three per cent of the Gallup poll who want America to keep the secret. But this can be said to any apostle of unlimited sovereignty: that in the world of weapons now being formed, life becomes so precarious as to rank unlimited sovereignty with the finest foolishness men have ever ventured to sponsor. People in such a world would indeed be living dangerously, in a danger never before equalled, and in a helplessness never before conceived. It is astonishing what atomic energy and guided missiles have made of the once reliable doctrine of unlimited sovereignty.

The man who plumps for world government has both logic and law on his side. And he makes no bones about it that it is the end result, not the next step, that interests him. He finds the world somewhat in the position of the American colonies after winning the war against England. The colonies had a confederation. Each colony was sovereign, and unwilling to limit its sovereignty. The world today has something like confederation in the United Nations, which also is an association of sovereign states. The assembly of the United Nations is not altogether unlike the Continental Congress of revolutionary days. That Congress had no power whatever, other than to approach the separate colonies with requests, pleas and exhortations. The confederation won a war, but it was not a government. The United Nations Organization is not a government. In one respect, the United Nations Organization is more powerful than the Continental Congress. It can operate against member states, with economic sanctions and then with military force. But even that does not make it a government. A government operates on individuals, not on states.

To go back to the debate which accompanied the transformation of our confederation to federal union; Madison argued that government must have the power to tax and to conscript. That is, it must be able to tax the individual and conscript the individual. And when our federal government was set up, it had these powers, along with many others. So, too, if we are to have world government, even of the most limited kind, it would have to operate against individuals. In the field of inspection alone—in controlling the making of weapons—it would have to have the power not only to enter factories and laboratories everywhere, it would have to have the power, too, to make arrests and to prosecute those who violate the law of the world organization. That is the test by which to measure proposals for turning over the atomic bomb to the Security Council, with power to inspect and control it. If the inspection and control are not against individuals, the proposals are not coming to grips with the problem. If they are against individuals, they are the beginning of world government and hence of the abolition of war.

In "The Talk of the Town" in the September 15 issue of the *New Yorker*, was this pertinent editorial: "As we listened to President Truman broadcasting his victory message to the troops on V-J Night, we wished he had included a paragraph or two from the article by Cord Meyer, Jr., in the current *Atlantic*. Meyer did a stretch with the United States Marines in the Pacific, and later with the United States delegates in San Francisco. Of the latter experience he wrote:

> I have described these provisions of the Charter because I wish to make one point so clear that no one can miss it. The International Organization cannot rely on its own power and authority in dealing with the most powerful nations of the world, because it has been given none. Behind the façade of what I believe to be genuinely good intentions, there remains the basic condition of anarchy implicit in the existence of absolutely independent nations with large amounts of armed force at their disposal.

"That," the *New Yorker* continues, "would have been a good passage to read to the troops just before Bing sang 'I'm Dreaming of a White Christmas.' It is this basic condition that the

United Nations Organization must hasten to improve," the editorial continues, "for as it is presently constituted, the organization has the authority of a yellow butterfly in a high wind. The people know this. The league must grow from league to union, (as the name United implies). It must grow and gain authority, first basically through the acquisition of federal power, then specifically through a proper use of this power. Then we can have all the white Christmases and international trials we want to. We can even have a law making it dangerous for any man to be inhuman to any other man."

CHAPTER V

No Defense

AMONG the numerous consultants of the United States delegation at the San Francisco Conference, selected and invited by the State Department, was not a single scientist invited because of his knowledge of science. Among the men invited to attend the educational meeting in London for the United States government, a meeting that was to set up an international education office, under the United Nations Organization, was not a single scientist invited because of his knowledge of science.

These two facts are about as symbolic as anything that can be said about the release of atomic energy having caught this country and its leaders incredulous and unprepared. Here we are on the threshold of the scientific era. That was known even before the atomic bomb was made. Social life will be transformed beyond recognition, and the architect of this future is not the statesman but the scientist. At San Francisco was being drafted the charter of the future world organization, which had to become the foundation of permanent peace, if it was to be worth anything. Yet not a single prophet of the century ahead of us was even asked to advise the men of state.

At the time of the San Francisco Conference the costly investment in making the atomic bomb was drawing to a close, and there were men in the government who knew about it. Obviously, the scientists familiar with nuclear physics could not have gone to San Francisco, and called attention to the work being done and its influence on the future. That would have been to tell the most astounding military secret of all history. But without revealing anything, or drawing attention to anything, the scientists might well have been quietly there to describe to the statesmen what kind of world they would live in, and for which they were drafting the charter of principles and the methods of procedure.

But they were not invited, and I am afraid it was not because of the need for secrecy about the atomic bomb, but simply because of obsolete thinking. And I am fortified in this view by the fact that no scientist of renown was invited to membership of the American delegation to the educational meeting. For now the existence of the atomic bomb is known, so secrecy is no longer an excuse. Many of our great research workers in science are also educators, and scientific education now becomes the dominant branch of it. It would be just as obsolete for educators to found an international education office without the expert consultation of scientists as for the governments to construct a world organization without it.

I am not arguing that the scientist, because he can split an atom, can also construct a world organization. The two functions are not comparable, and splitting the atom is in a different dimension of achievement. But a scientist who knows what can be expected from an atomic bomb can tell the statesman that it doesn't make much sense to build a world organization that allows for war, since war in the atomic era will destroy civilization. Well, nobody told the sages at San Francisco anything of the kind, and they went ahead and built a world organization that is suited only to the preatomic era, and has no validity in the atomic age.

What do the scientists think about this today? What do they think of their handiwork? They made the bomb, the bomb has slain its tens of thousands, and they have an inescapable responsibility. It is the responsibility of the scientists toward mankind whom they serve—and they do consider themselves servants of mankind. Dr. Samuel K. Allison, head of the Institute of Nuclear Studies of the University of Chicago, made a statement at a luncheon of seventeen scientists in Chicago—all men who had worked on the bomb—in which he said: "All of us had a momentary elation when our experiment met with success, but that feeling rapidly changed to a feeling of horror and a fervent hope that no more bombs would be dropped. When the second bomb was released, we felt it was a greater tragedy." He said he had hoped that we would merely show the Japanese that we had so much power, by dropping an atomic bomb on an unoccupied island or in Japanese home waters. "It was a real tragedy," he said, "that such an important discovery, that may bring about unbelievable changes in the world was introduced to the public thus."

This statement appeared at first in only one edition of the New York *Herald Tribune,* but later was quoted by Dorothy Thompson in her column. And it raises the question of what scientists who made the bomb think, not only of the way it was introduced, but of what it means to the world of the future. We know from several protests that they chafe under the strict government control which continues to be exercised, and want to get back to their research work in their own laboratories. For bomb-making is the smaller part of the development of nuclear physics. All the sciences will be fertilized by the fission of the atom in some way or other, and the atomic era now opening is still before its dawn. We can hardly imagine what it will bring in full noon light.

The scientists who made the bomb have concrete ideas about the social implications of what they have done. A typical document that has been drawn up by scientists who worked and are still working on the atomic bomb expresses the views prevailing in the whole body of scientists who worked on the project. These scientists, in three parts of the country, met and discussed their problems, and separately arrived at the same general conclusions.

"They have," says the document, "been thinking about this situation for a considerably longer time than was possible for the public. We feel that it is our duty to present to the public the basic facts concerning the atomic bomb and their implications for United States foreign policy. Only by a full realization of these facts can the citizens of the country intelligently participate in making the decisions that the unleashing of atomic energy compels us to take. If wrong decisions are made, it may mean the destruction of our cities, horrible death for millions of our people, and possibly the end of our nation."

The document proceeds with an analysis of the courses that might be followed. One is to make no change in our present international relations. This, it says, is based on the argument that the atomic bomb is not a development great enough to change the nature of war, that an effective defense is sure to be found, and that moral pressure and the fear of retaliation will prevent its use, or prevent war altogether. As scientists who made it, the writers of the document speak with authority about the power of the bomb. "By using more bombs, larger bombs, and more efficient bombs," they say, "it will be possible in the near future to destroy completely the bulk of the population, industry and military strength of any nation within a few weeks. Aviation and rocket developments might enable this to be accomplished within a few hours, without possibility of effective retaliation. Strategic locations may be mined in advance by agents of foreign governments."

The scientists proceed to state as experts that: "We can offer no hope of a specific defense against the atomic bomb. The only immediate defense measures are retaliation, counter-offensive or preventive warfare." They note that moral considerations did not prevent the use of the bomb against Japan, and that the Allied people have, to a large extent, approved the decision to use it. So we are led to assume that moral sanctions will not keep it from being used. Nor do they believe the fear of retaliation will do so. "Fear of being subjected to atomic bomb attacks may, in fact," they say, "enhance the possibility that a nation itself will use them as a preventive measure."

In view of these factors, the scientists reject the idea that we need not change our present foreign policy. That leads them to examine other alternatives. One is that we can keep the bomb a secret. Here again they speak as experts, and what they say must be given fullest respect. This is their declaration, as it is worded:

"There are no longer any fundamental secrets about the atomic bomb. The government has made public the broad outline of the discovery and methods which led to success. The remaining 'secrets' are scientific and engineering details. Even those nations with lesser resources than those of the United States will be able to produce atomic bombs within two to five years."

Keeping the bomb a secret has two bad consequences, they state. It spurs other nations to develop atomic bombs, and it sterilizes the further development of nuclear physics and chemistry in this country. Further, Anglo-American control of raw material necessary to make the bomb is impossible. Hence, they say, we might have to work on making more and better bombs. But having more and better bombs, they point out, is no defense. "Once a nation possesses a certain minimum number of bombs, there is no great advantage in having more. Within a few years, a nation with a small number of atomic bombs carried by rockets or planted as mines in our cities, could, in a few minutes, destroy most of the industrial resources of the United States and much of its population."

The last remaining defense would be dispersal of population and industries, which would be only a partial defense, and which, they believe, might not be possible without totalitarian government.

So they come to yet another alternative. Since we shall not have the bombs exclusively for more than five years, and no adequate defense against them thereafter, we might set out to conquer the world within the next five years. And this, naturally, they dismiss as a course of action not much different from that of the Nazis.

So they arrive, inevitably, at the final conclusion that there must be international control of atomic power, which they call the only real and possible long-term solution. "The people of the United States, together with the peoples of the rest of the world," they say, "must demand that their leaders work together to find means of effective international co-operation on atomic power. They must not fail. The alternatives lead to world suicide."

And Dr. J. R. Oppenheimer, who directed the making of the bomb, added one more thought. "Our great problem," he said, "is the prevention of war, and the peaceful use of atomic power." To which I may be permitted to add: There is no time to lose.

CHAPTER VI

Mr. Truman's Difficult Decision

P RESIDENT TRUMAN's message to Congress about
what to do with the atomic bomb represents one of the greatest
responsibilities ever entrusted to a single person in the history
of man's social life on this planet. And I ask you to contemplate
the responsibility and the man who has to bear it.

When President Roosevelt died, and Harry Truman became
President, his first thoughts may well have been that he was
taking over as pilot on a voyage whose course already was set,
and he had at most to see it through, and so to complete, rather
than to create. There is no doubt that the new President felt
reverence for the creative genius of the man whose work he
was to fulfill. It is a fair assumption that it did not at first occur
to President Truman—who is a humble man—that the responsibilities which were to weigh on him and challenge his own
creative genius were equal to those met by President Roosevelt,
or perhaps even heavier. One can imagine what took place in his
mind when he realized he must make the fateful decision about
the use of the atomic bomb. No single decision in the career of
Franklin Roosevelt was comparable in gravity with this. And
there he was, Harry Truman, less than four months Vice President, and suddenly become President, who must decide by
himself and indeed in the solitude of his soul and in humility
before God, the commencement of a new era.

The decision to use the bomb was not the hardest decision in
the matter, but it was hard enough. Harry Truman is a man
of good will and conscience, as are the rank and file of American
people. To decide to use, for the death of innumerable enemy

civilians, a weapon placed in one's control by destiny is no easy decision. And President Truman knew that he would be judged for what he decided, by his contemporaries, by history, and by the Judge beyond all judges.

He made the decision that the bomb should be used. He has been criticized for the way it was used. He may be criticized as long as the history of these times is written. But he will be justified by the consideration that he was responsible for the lives of Americans in war time, before he was answerable for the lives of the Japanese. That is the code of war and we were at war.

But having made that fateful choice, President Truman could hardly let it rest there. It was a grim choice and a dreadful one for a man of good will and conscience. It could only be vindicated by a further decision that the new era of atomic energy must be an era of peace, and that in this era, the United States must pioneer.

It was ten days after the bomb had been set off in New Mexico, which meant that we had the weapon, and were going to use it, that President Truman stood before the audience of fellow Missourians in Kansas City to receive the honorary degree of Doctor of Laws from Kansas City University. He spoke extemporaneously. So what he said could either reveal the train of his own thoughts, or hide it. As you know, it was a speech of revelation. As he was being given a Doctorate of Law, his mind turned to law. "We live," he said, "in an age of law and an age of reason, an age in which we can get along with our neighbors. Now, we must do that nationally. It will be just as easy for nations to get along in a republic of the world as it is for you to get along in the Republic of the United States." After winning the war with Japan, the President said, "We must win the peace of the world. And unless *we* lead the way, there will be no peace in the world." These are the thoughts to which his mind turned ten days after the New Mexico explosion.

As I was saying, the decision to use the bomb in warfare was not the hardest one to make. The hardest one comes now. It is what to do with the atomic bomb now that the war has ended, when the existence of the bomb overshadows every other consideration in the planning of security and the conduct of foreign relations.

The release of atomic energy, in its first practical form, may be too overwhelming an event for you and me, as unscientific laymen, to appreciate fully. But President Truman, though he also is an unscientific layman, had a political decision to make, not a scientific one. And in politics he is no layman. He knows enough about nuclear physics to know that man stands before the millennium, and that he stands also before destruction. It may take decades, or dozens of decades to achieve the millennium of unlimited prosperity in the midst of lasting peace. The destruction may come in a single decade or two. And what he, President Harry Truman, decides will go far toward influencing which it is that man is to experience.

Put that way, as a plain choice between the millennium and destruction, you might think it is an easy choice to make. Well, look back to President Roosevelt. He also faced a simple choice: Should we prepare to defend the United States and to defeat the forces of enslavement and aggression, or should we be indifferent to a conquest of Hitler in Europe and of Japanese militarism in Asia. But it took skill, leadership, and mastery of techniques, as well as vision, to bring us through to the final victory. And it will take all these qualities if we are to have a science-made millennium instead of destruction.

So the task of President Truman, though different, in no way is less than that of President Roosevelt. And one can well conceive of it as being still more formidable. President Truman has more to do than finish the work of President Roosevelt. He has to initiate a new design of living for the human family. The design worked out in the Roosevelt era is not adequate. Without their knowing it, or being able to know it, the statesmen who drafted the Charter at San Francisco, were drafting something that in ten years will belong in a museum.

Since his speech at Kansas City, President Truman has made two more revelations of the direction of his thoughts. One was at a press conference in which someone sounded him out on isolationism. He was told of an opinion that the American people are in a more isolationist mood than they were a little while ago. Quick as a flash the President said he did not agree, and added that if we ever get to that point, we would be on the road to ruin, just as in 1920. So, as far as the bomb is concerned, the President obviously is not thinking that our possession of it and having the so-called secret is going to make it safe for us to be isolationists.

But even more revealing is a remark the President made at an informal press conference on his return from his Annapolis weekend. Its importance must be read in connection with reports of a cabinet discussion on the atomic bomb. The newspapers gave totally different versions of what was said at that discussion, and who said it. The first version was that Secretary Wallace had come out in favor of disclosing the secret to the Soviet Union, to which the rest of the cabinet demurred. President Truman himself denied the accuracy of this version.

Another version, obviously produced to refute the first one, is that Secretary Stimson had written a memorandum proposing that the atomic bomb should be turned over to the United Nations Organization under certain conditions, and that Secretary Wallace and Acting Secretary Fortas at the cabinet meeting supported him. The remainder of the cabinet—like the great majority of Congressmen so far polled in the matter—were reported to be for keeping the so-called "secret." President Truman said significantly to the newspaper men that, like Lincoln, he must make the decision himself, whether or not his cabinet agreed with him. And he said he was thinking of Lincoln's decision, against the advice of his cabinet, to issue the Emancipation Proclamation.

It took courage for Lincoln to issue the Emancipation Proclamation, which is now one of the beloved mileposts on the progress of man toward freedom. And if the President has such thoughts in connection with his own decision, he obviously has the courage to face making an equally brave and historic decision. This is said not to imply that the President, when he sends his message to Congress, will show that he expects to reach the millennium at a single leap, for, as I said, he is a political expert. He must take first steps first.

One thing the President knows is that he needs more than his own stoutness of soul, and more than his own prayers. In that Kansas City speech, made ten days after the epochal explosion in New Mexico, he said: "I have a tremendous task, one that I dare not look too closely at to understand, for the simple reason that no man can do it by himself. I must have the wholehearted and unqualified support of the country to win the Japanese war, and then to win the peace."

So the President in those days of soul-searching, acknowledged that he could not lead unless he expressed and fulfilled what the American people want. He was learning anew the principle of President Roosevelt's power.

President Truman can hear the ringing call of the very scientists who made the bomb that a world order must be created which alone can control it for constructive uses. He has the encouragement of the veteran organizations dedicated to the study of foreign relations, who agree that a world organization must be evolved which alone has the use of aggressive weapons. They propose steps of differing lengths to arrive at this limited world government. But they see the same goal. And he knows quite well he has only a few years, if the world foundation is to be laid in time.

The decision he announces in his message to Congress, unless it is to be a product of cynical jingoism, or of fevered bigotry, will have to win its way with the help of the basic wisdom of rank and file Americans. These rank and file Americans fought the war and know the folly of war. They are deeply troubled by the rising rivalries of the postwar world, and by the very magnitude of the destructive power now almost within general grasp. These Americans, along with President Truman, must have the courage to enter the future and shape for it a new relationship of nations.

CHAPTER VII

The President's Message

IN WRITING his message on the atomic bomb, President Truman divided his subject into two parts, domestic and international. The international part was what the public was most interested in. As it turned out, it was only in this part that the President was cautious and inconclusive. He contented himself with a promise to try to get the use of the bomb in wartime outlawed, and to obtain international co-operation for a peacetime use of atomic energy.

It was the domestic part of the message which proved to be revolutionary. For it sets up a pattern for government control and supervision of what may be a main source of power in the future. This may not have been appraised at its true value because twice in the message the President spoke appreciatively of private enterprise, and he seemed to be telling Congress that it must so legislate as to give private enterprise what it had had in the past.

But in fact he was saying nothing of the kind. He was saying that in the vast atomic experiment the United States Government has set up a huge establishment with a gifted personnel, which now must be kept together. He was saying that a government commission should be named with power to control this establishment. It must have, as well, the control and supervision of all land and mineral deposits owned by the United States which constitute sources of atomic energy, and all stockpiles of materials from which such energy may be derived, and all plants or other property of the United States connected with its development.

Further, the commission is to be authorized to acquire by purchase or condemnation any minerals or other materials from which the sources of atomic energy can be derived, and also any land containing such minerals or materials which are not already owned by the United States. The commission is to conduct all necessary research, experimentation and operations for the further development and use of atomic energy for all purposes —military, industrial, scientific or medical. And finally, under proper safeguards the commission shall be permitted to license any property available to the commission for research, development and exploitation in the field of atomic energy. Of course, said the President, such licensing should be conditioned upon a policy of widespread distribution of peacetime products on equitable terms which will prevent monopoly.

And finally, the President recommended that to establish effective control and security, it should be declared unlawful to produce or use the substances comprising the sources of atomic energy, or to import or export them except under conditions prescribed by the commission.

In quoting these passages I have left out the references to private enterprise. They simply say that since our science and industry owe their strength to the spirit of free inquiry and the spirit of free enterprise, the commission is to interfere as little as possible with private research and private enterprise, and should use, as much as possible, existing private and public institutions and agencies. Later the injunction is repeated to say that in developing atomic energy for all purposes, the committee is to use existing private and public institutions. But if the rest of the message is grasped one sees that while the President makes his bow to private enterprise, it is for what it has achieved in the past, not for what it will achieve in the domain of atomic energy in the future. And he himself was aware of what he was saying, for he wrote that the measures which he had suggested might seem drastic and far-reaching, but that the discovery with which we are dealing involves forces of nature too dangerous to fit into any of our usual concepts.

What he does is to lay down the basic principle that there must be strong government supervision of something so far-reaching in its possible effects and benefits. Private enterprise is to be used. It is even to dispense atomic energy under license. But it can do nothing with it except under conditions prescribed by the commission. And this is the logical next step after the government brought together the scientists and the engineers, the workmen and the industrialists, and produced a result that none of them could have produced singly. It is quite correct to say that private enterprise was essential in the process. But private enterprise was utterly incapable of handling so large an assignment by itself. In fact, it went into it with the greatest reluctance and indeed disbelief. It really had to be commandeered by the final persuasiveness of patriotism. President Truman makes it quite clear that he is not turning his back on free enterprise. But in the field of atomic energy, it is not to have the role it has enjoyed before. And this is not because free enterprise has in any way failed; it is because our social organization has been overtaken by a development so profoundly revolutionary that it must be altered to meet it.

And in meeting it, President Truman sets up a formula which may well be what the world has waited for—a formula that combines private enterprise with government control and supervision, without retaining predatory capitalism of the old kind, on the one hand, or going into totalitarianism on the other. Since there is to be freedom of enterprise, the civil liberties essential to this freedom can be preserved. Since there is to be government control, the public interest can be safeguarded. And one dimly sees the vista of a world made healthy and prosperous by science, but without sacrifice of its freedoms.

In one further respect President Truman takes a clear and important line. His commission, which is to control atomic energy, is a civilian, not a military commission. So the development of the energy for peaceful purposes is given precedence over its development for war. It is not to be held back because of possible use in war. The easy argument of national security—

or international security—is not being used to vest in the Army this tremendous power over civilian life.

This is important for the fact that if the Army were to keep control, and private enterprise were to be used wherever possible, the partnership of big business with the Army would be a menace to our political institutions. Big business and the Army got along together splendidly during the war, and that was all to the good, in wartime. But in the peace we do not dare submit our civilization to this partnership. It is far too powerful, and by its very nature it is indifferent to individual and social requirements. It is not of the essence of democracy. But a civilian commission, dedicated to the public good, and serving under the ultimate control of the representatives of the people, can be of the essence of democracy.

The Truman proposal, then, sets up three invaluable principles. It ranks the civilian, peacetime contribution of the release of atomic energy ahead of its military use, it assigns to scientists themselves a social responsibility that measures up to their scientific contribution, and it gives government the unique place it must fill in the times ahead, a place of control which does not endanger the freedoms already won and established.

Attention now will focus on the legislation before Congress to set up this commission, and then on the appointments to it. No more significant or powerful commission will have been created in this country in modern times. Obviously the greatest watchfulness needs to be shown to prevent any dilution of the President's principles in writing the new statute. For far-sighted men of ambition will see how great are the powers at stake, and quite naturally they will work as effectively and as quietly as they can to lay hands on them. That is the nature of the democratic struggle, and it takes just as much foresight by the people themselves to keep command of their own destinies.

When the commission is set up, it must be as aware as is the President himself that it faces a drastic task, that it is pushing back frontiers, not preserving an old and a limited system, that in its keeping is the safe evolution of the greatest of all revolutions, if its members are mature enough and we are mature enough to go confidently forward and have the revolution in social safety. It is a colossal responsibility, and one would be hard put to it to name six or eight Americans on whose wisdom and fitness for such a task there would be national agreement.

The President cannot be criticized for not being as revolutionary in the international part of his message. Congress is not ready to follow a lead for the early establishment of that Republic of the World to which Mr. Truman referred in his Kansas City speech. Congress will not be ready for that until it has felt the pressure of American public opinion, and felt it strongly and for some time. President Roosevelt was master of the art of timing, and particularly of knowing when to go into active leadership. It was his rule to do it when he knew he had enough of a following. President Truman may be showing mastery of the same art. He said nothing about international use of the bomb that is inconsistent with a later attempt to abolish war by putting *all* aggressive weapons in possession of a world government. But he also said nothing more than faintly recognizing the dire need for such a government.

He said that a new force has been constituted that is too revolutionary to consider in the framework of old ideas. He acknowledged that we can no longer rely on the slow progress of time to develop a program of control among nations. He saw that civilization demands that we shall reach at the earliest possible date a satisfactory arrangement for the control of this discovery. But then he cut down his thinking to a meager proposal that there should be a renunciation of the use and development of the atomic bomb, and this he is now to try to obtain by early negotiations.

The greatest persuasion we might have had not to have the bomb used against us would have been not to have used it ourselves. We used it to save lives. If there is another war, and other nations use rocket bombs, crop-destroying gases, disease germs, or what other dreadful weapons there may be, are we sure we should not use the atomic bomb again? To be effective President Truman's negotiations must include *all* the new weapons. And the problem then becomes one of the control of *all* aggressive weapons, and that can only be done for certain through a government with power to control them.

If President Truman had thought Congress already knew this, he undoubtedly would have said it. Since he did not say it, he is waiting for public opinion to take the lead. If and when enough Americans are in favor of *abolishing* war, they can launch this nation on the moral leadership of the world and probably achieve their end.

CHAPTER VIII

The May-Johnson Bill

IN ANNOUNCING that we are to keep the atomic bomb a secret, President Truman has definitely put us into atomic competition with the Soviet Union. In effect he says: "We are ahead; we intend to stay ahead." So in effect he is saying that we are not committed to build a world in which the atomic bomb will not be made and used, but are committing our security to force, rather than agreement, and to the power to kill rather than the power to reason. Atomic competition is the modern word for armament competition.

President Truman has made a grave decision. One could search through all our past and indeed through history without coming up with many, if any, more grave. Fortunately, it is not an irrevocable decision. Fortunately, we are a democracy, and the President and the Congress are subject to the will of the people. When this will comes to be expressed, nothing could be more unexpected than to find that the American people wish an armament race with the Soviet Union, or are resigned to anticipate the war which ends all armament races. It is not the American way to believe that the world should be ruled by the power to kill rather than the power to reason.

President Truman admits that the secret of the atomic bomb is chiefly in the engineering "know-how." He and General Groves are of the opinion that this cannot be mastered by the Soviet Union for many years. It is that which puts us ahead in the race for power. This is a shift from the earlier thesis that there are profound scientific secrets not available to research workers in other lands. Our own scientists have bluntly scotched that idea. People measuring Russia's industrial know-how do not always recognize what has been accomplished in the Soviet Union in the past few years, and can be expected under Russian impetus alone in the next few years. But what is also to the point, they ignore the fact that the Germans have engineering know-how to a high degree. True, the Germans did not develop the atomic bomb first. They made some mistakes our scientists avoided—perhaps only a single one of importance. But if they were behind in that, they were ahead with other revolutionary weapons not perfected in this country. The German know-how still exists. Much of the best scientific and engineering work done in Germany was in the occupation zone held by the Russians. The Russians are not overlooking anything. One can be sure that they are already in touch with the best German scientists and engineers. And our safe lead may not last as long as we think. On examination it becomes a slender reed on which to build our national safety.

In October 1945, Congressional hearings began over a set of some of the most important bills ever to be introduced in its history. One set—the Magnuson and Kilgore bills—has to do with the government's fostering, financing and guiding the scientific education and research in this country. The other—the May-Johnson bill—is for the control of atomic energy in this country, a bill presumed to implement the recommendations in the President's atomic bomb message. If anyone has the idea that we are preparing to enter the scientific era in a big way, and in a wise way, he should study the bills and do a little private figuring. Curiously enough, the witnesses heard on the bills have not been critical on the score that we are doing too little to take advantage of what science offers. We still regard science as a useful sideshow, even in these bills. And it is indeed too little, if we are, as President Truman has announced, to keep the bomb a secret, and thus invite competition from weapons that will be kept secret from us.

Before the war, the expenditure on pure and applied science in this country, by all agencies, governmental, industrial and by public foundations, came to between two and three cents out of every hundred dollars of national income. It rose during the war. The government alone spent at the rate of forty-four cents of every hundred dollars of national income on pure and applied science in the year 1944. But if after the war is spent all told as much as the government spent at the peak, plus what all private spenders spent, the total will hardly come to more than sixty cents of every hundred dollars of national income. I don't know how much the Russians are going to spend of their national income on science. I don't know how large their national income is. But the Russians are going for science in a much more basic and sweeping way than we are. They might decide to spend ten cents on every dollar of income, or even twenty cents on the dollar. That would be spectacular, but the Russians are able to concentrate effort in this way. If they spend ten cents on the dollar and we spend six cents on the hundred dollars, the Russians would be spending at a rate more than sixteen times greater than ours. So it is a question of great urgency, and one on which the scientists should be heard, and the public should have the most thorough education. We must know whether we are doing anything like as much as we must do to keep our leadership in the scientific world. The bit of engineering know-how which is our margin of safety today might dwindle to less than nothing, if the Russians should decide to marshal their resources and effort in a big way.

As I said, this point was not raised in the hearings in Washington. What one heard most about was controls. And this issue arose over the Magnuson and Kilgore bills. These are the bills having to do with scientific education and research, and which carry out the recommendations of Dr. Vannevar Bush's celebrated report, called "Science, the Endless Frontier." The Magnuson bill provides for control by a board of nine members serving without compensation. The Kilgore bill provides for control by a single administrator, responsible to the President and served by an advisory council of eight government officials plus eight public members. On its face, the difference between the two bills looks like a difference between one man and eight, with the greater safety lying in the eight. But that is not the case. But this question of control in the two bills on scientific research and education is simply the tip-off of the far more fundamental problem of the control of atomic energy as set forth in the May-Johnson bill.

All that was said about who shall control research and education is just a preview of what should be said about the control of atomic energy itself. It matters what happens in controlling the field of education and research. But what happens in controlling the field of atomic energy matters so much more it is difficult to find temperate language to express it. As the May-Johnson bill is now drawn, the control is vested in a way that might become a perfected Fascist domination of our economic life. Certainly there is nothing in the bill to prevent it. There is everything to encourage it. It is therefore the most ominous of bills. And this question who is to control our entry into the scientific era involves issues that are the most important of our times, if not in our history.

Let me remind you that President Truman's message on the control of atomic energy was an admirable document, so far as its recommendations for the domestic control of atomic energy are concerned. It set the use of atomic energy for civilian life ahead of its military use. It proposed a control by civilians for the general good. It provided government controls of great powers, but also assured the proper use of atomic energy by private enterprise. And thus it might have been the guide for the drafting of a model bill laying down the principles of a mixed government-private enterprise economy in the scientific era.

But the May-Johnson bill which purports to implement its principles is a shrewd and astonishing measure, if for only one stipulation in it. That is as to control. The atomic energy commission is to consist of nine members, to be chosen by the President with advice and consent of the Senate. Once appointed, they cannot be removed by the President before the end of their terms, except for inability to act, neglect of duty, malfeasance in office, conflict of interests, or because continuance in office would be inimical to the national interest. These are precise grounds, and leave out of account that a member simply may be behaving in a way that has aroused public dissatisfaction, and therefore should be removable by the President for the good of the country, and not because he has done something wrong.

"Members of the commission," says the bill, "may engage in other occupations or business, private or governmental, to an extent not inconsistent with the performance of their duties, and may hold other offices or positions under the United States and receive compensation therefor." Members of the commission are to be paid only fifty dollars for every day actually spent on their duties. This may sound ultra-innocent. But it is the opposite, if one goes on to read that to this commission will be given powers over all atomic research, over all source materials, with power to make any cost-plus contracts, to license the use of atomic energy, to buy, lease and hold property, and to dispose of it, to exercise the right of eminent domain and many other powers. It will control completely the creation of atomic energy and its disposal, this power which today still belongs to the people.

What is there to prevent the nine commissioners from being in fact representatives of nine vast corporations? They do not even need to sever their corporation connections to serve. And once in command of the basic power resource of the country—which atomic energy may well be—they could dominate the country. The nine commissioners might thus become the nine pillars of a corporative state. And that is the name for one kind of a Fascist state. The President, as we have seen, cannot easily remove them. So the public cannot have them removed through pressure on the President. In this way, atomic energy can be turned over to private interests with hardly any protection of the public to whom it now belongs.

The May-Johnson bill was given one day of public hearings by the House Committee on Military Affairs, and only four witnesses were heard. The scientists who worked on the atomic bomb are demanding an opportunity to present to the public just what is involved in the release of atomic energy. The scientists know about atomic power. Obviously there are some men in Washington who know about political power. Atomic power is so great that it frightens the sanest man. But so is the political power, and it is high time to be disturbed by what is happening.

CHAPTER IX

"And Now Come the Scientists"

IN THE wake of the atomic bomb, which they created, came the scientists, almost as in a procession, marching upon the stage of public affairs, and for the first time in their lives taking a lead in guiding the nation. It is to be hoped that the scientists, now that they have found their way to the Congressional committee rooms and press conferences, will continue this kind of public service. They have proved to be as impressive a group of men as ever came to modern Washington.

It somewhat astonished Washington to find that so many of these scientists—these secluded masters of intensive research—are young men—in the middle thirties. Their hair is not long. Their faces are open and clear, their eyes look steadily, and as witnesses before the Senate and House committees, and in their newspaper conferences, they were quiet, modest, lucid and compellingly convincing. They know what they are talking about. These are the men who know what the atomic bomb can do. You and I have to imagine it, if we can, and transform our habits of thinking accordingly. But these scientists have been at this work of bomb-making and atom-splitting for some time. They know as a scientific possibility something that you and I cannot well taken in, and that is that in five, ten or twenty years a great part of the population of this country might not be here, that some dire day or night it might be wiped out. As one witness put it before a Senate committee, it is quite possible that 40,000,000 Americans, those living in cities, might be gone in a single day.

The scientists are to be congratulated on obtaining the reopening of the hearings on the May-Johnson bill for control of atomic energy. The bulk of the evidence was against the bill, though Dr. J. R. Oppenheimer did speak for it, on the ground that some bill is needed to get rid of present military control. But he also said it would have to be changed ultimately, and he called it too sweeping. At the risk of making too sweeping a generalization, let me say that the scientists seem to fear an administration of atomic energy in peacetime under the same General Groves who had command of the atomic project during the war. They foresee his being given the job with a navy man as deputy administrator. That disturbs them as much as the nine commissioners at a dollar a year who might turn out to be representatives of the big corporations, and who, with the wide powers of the bill, might develop into dictators of our national economy. The scientists are concerned to avert a dictatorship by General Groves, or any other military figure, though they are not conducting a personal campaign against the general. In a formal statement, the Atomic Scientists of Chicago and the Association of Oak Ridge Scientists at Clinton Laboratories, gave their reasons for opposing the May-Johnson bill. "It delegates," they say, "to a commission and an administrator, not responsible to the electorate, the authority and duty of determining and formulating, in addition to enforcing, all national policy in regard to atomic energy. Neither the commission nor the administrator is responsible to the President or any other authority. Further, they are virtually immune from outside criticism or review, because their security regulations may prevent the disclosure of the actions or policies subject to criticism."

It came out in the Congressional hearings that in the making of the bomb during the war, the scientists, who were kept compartmented under strictest security rules, actually had to break the rules and tell each other what they were doing so as to get ahead with the work. That is, they had to risk their jobs so as to do their jobs. The same kind of secrecy could prevail under the same administrator by the terms of the bill. Here are some of the objections they noted: "Under the broad powers contained in the bill," they say, "the proposed commission or administrator selected by it may restrict all scientific and industrial research to government agencies, may place no restrictions whatever on such research, or may take an intermediary policy." Obviously, the scientists believe the bill should be specific.

Here is another respect in which they believe the bill gives too much power: "In new fields whose importance to our economic life cannot yet be foreseen," they say, "the proposed commission and the administrator may completely ban private enterprise, or may completely turn over development, exploitation and patents to private interests."

A further grant of power they criticize is that the commission "may allow full and complete revelation of all present and future knowledge, or may promulgate security regulations so stringent as to prevent the discussion and interchange of information, the life-blood of scientific progress, even between co-workers in the same laboratory, public or private. The scope of the regulations," they point out, "is not limited to those necessary for military security." They criticize the bill for making possible the appointment as administrator and deputy administrator of officers on active duty in the armed forces, who would then be responsible for the administration of both military and non-military aspects of atomic energy.

> We believe [they conclude], that there is great danger under the proposed bill of retarding the research and development of atomic energy.
>
> As citizens and as scientists who have worked to bring to fruition the promise of atomic energy, we believe that controls should and must be exercised by an administrative agency of the government. The controls must be exercised for the military security and general welfare of our people, subject to international agreements for the preservation of world peace. We believe, however, that the limits and objectives of these controls must be defined by the people through their elected Congress. This may be accomplished only by a law drafted after the fullest discussion, in Congress and out,

of the meaning and possibilities of atomic energy and atomic bombs. It requires full presentation of the views of the armed forces, scientists, industry, commerce, labor, agriculture and others whose lives and interests will be affected.

We propose that the present bill be abandoned, and that steps be taken to prepare a new bill based on extended hearings and investigation. It should embody enforceable objectives and limitations on the controls to be exercised. If the demands for continuity of the work and military security require immediate action, we propose that Congress pass interim legislation enabling work and security to be carried on for six months in the present wartime manner.

Many of the witnesses heard were impressive, but none more so than Dr. Oppenheimer, called the outstanding atomic bomb expert of the nation, and Dr. H. J. Curtis, leader in the Oak Ridge project. On the political consequences of the bomb, they left no doubt that they see mankind having to choose between world co-operation and destruction. That, I believe, has been the view expressed without exception by the scientists who have worked on the bomb. They may differ as to the precise form of the world co-operation, but not as to the choice. To the inevitable question by a Congressman: "Isn't it visionary?" Dr. Curtis replied: "I will simply state that the possibility of developing atomic energy was also labeled visionary a scant six years ago. Today it is a reality. We can see no reason," he continued, "why a similar miracle cannot be achieved in international relations."

The scientists swept away two widely believed myths with their testimony. One is that there is a defense against the bomb. Hardly a week passes without some story coming along—one or two from Navy sources—saying that a defense against the bomb has been perfected. No wonder the Navy is anxious on the subject, for it is no secret that the bomb has made essential a re-assessment of the whole field of naval power and warfare. Dr. Oppenheimer said quietly: "Our bombs cannot be exploded before they reach their destination . . . Many persons," he continued, "squirm and try to say there is a counter-measure. There never will be a counter-measure against the atomic bomb, although there may be a way to intercept the bomb carriers." Dr. Curtis agreed. "We can," he said, "offer no hope of a specific defense against the atomic bomb. Nor will counter-offensive warfare restore the ruins of our cities, or revive the millions of our dead."

The other myth they disposed of is the secrecy of the bomb. "It is no secret at all to the scientists of other nations," said Dr. Oppenheimer. "Its production by other nations is only a matter of time and no very long time at that, not more than a few years probably for some of them. From the armament race that would most certainly follow, the United States might or might not emerge as winner, nor would it greatly matter. It is not necessary for a nation to be able to produce more or bigger or better bombs, but only to decide to proceed independently with its own atom bomb program, after which with very few bombs it could put any other nation, our own included, out of action." The most disconcerting thing Dr. Oppenheimer said was that while we have the temporary advantage the advent of atomic power has weakened the military position of the United States, because we live in such congregated areas.

Keeping the bomb a secret is, as I have said, launching an atomic competition with the Soviet Union. We start the race ahead of the Russians. But we are and will continue to be more vulnerable than they are. *We* cannot be made safe unless some form of international organization is created that prevents aggressive wars. That is the only complete safety. No one can have taken in what scientists said in Washington without seeing that this not only is logical, but the one realistic assurance of secure life.

CHAPTER X

Dr. Einstein on World Government

It WAS my privilege to make public a statement by Dr. Albert Einstein on the political consequences of the release of atomic energy. The statement is one that Dr. Einstein made to me at his home in Princeton, and which was published in the November issue of the *Atlantic Monthly*. Dr. Einstein's theories are the foundation of nuclear physical research, and his letter to President Roosevelt in 1939 was the instigation of the great research and production task which ended in the manufacture of the atomic bomb.

The release of atomic energy [Dr. Einstein told me], has not created a new problem. It has merely made more urgent the necessity of solving an existing one. One could say, that it has affected us quantitatively, not qualitatively. As long as there are sovereign nations possessing great power, war is inevitable. That statement is not an attempt to say when war will come, but only that it is sure to come. That fact was true before the atomic bomb was made. What has been changed is the destructiveness of war. I do not believe that civilization will be wiped out in a war fought with the atomic bomb. Perhaps two-thirds of the people of the earth might be killed, but enough men capable of thinking, and enough books, would be left to start again, and civilization could be restored.

I do not believe that the secret of the bomb should be given to the United Nations Organization. I do not believe that it should be given to the Soviet Union. Either course would be like the action of a man with capital, who, wishing another man to work with him on some enterprise, should start out by simply giving his prospective partner half of his money. The second man might choose to start a rival enterprise, when what was wanted was his co-operation.

The secret of the bomb should be committed to a World Government, and the United States should immediately announce its readiness to give it to a World Government. This government should be founded by the United States, the Soviet Union, and Great Britain—the only three powers with great military strength. All three of them should commit to this World Government all of their military strength. The fact that there are only three nations with great military power should make it easier rather than harder to establish such a government.

Since the United States and Great Britain have the secret of the atomic bomb and the Soviet Union does not, they should invite the Soviet Union to prepare and present the first draft of a Constitution for the proposed World Government. That action should help to dispel the distrust which the Russians already feel because the bomb is being kept a secret, chiefly to prevent their having it. Obviously the first draft would not be the final one, but the Russians should be made to feel that the World Government would assure them their security.

It would be wise if this Constitution were to be negotiated by a single American, a single Britisher and a single Russian. They would have to have advisers, but these advisers should only advise when asked. I believe three men can succeed in writing a workable constitution acceptable to all three nations. Six or seven men, or more, probably would fail.

After the three great powers have drafted a Constitution and adopted it, the smaller nations should be invited to join the World Government. They should be free to stay out; and though they would be perfectly secure in staying out, I am sure they would wish to join. Naturally they should be entitled to propose changes in the constitution as drafted by the Big Three. But the Big Three should go ahead and organize the World Government whether the smaller nations join or not. The World Government would have power over all military matters and need have only one further power: the power to intervene in countries where a minority is oppressing a majority and creating the kind of instability that leads to war. Conditions such as exist in Argentina and Spain should be dealt with. There must be an end to the concept of non-intervention, for to end it is part of keeping the peace.

The establishment of the World Government must not have to wait until the same conditions of freedom are to be found in all three of the great powers. While it is true that in the Soviet Union the minority rules, I do not consider that internal conditions there are of themselves a threat to world peace. One must bear in mind that the people in Russia did not have a long political education, and changes to improve Russian conditions had to be carried through by a minority for the reason that there was no majority capable of doing it. If I had been born a Russian, I believe I could have adjusted myself to this condition.

Do I fear the tyranny of a World Government? Of course I do. But I fear still more the coming of another war or wars. Any government is certain to be evil to some extent. But a World Government is preferable to the far greater evil of wars, particularly with their intensified destructiveness. If a World Government is not established by agreement, I believe it will come in another way and in a much more dangerous form. For war or wars will end in one power's being supreme and dominating the rest of the world by its overwhelming military strength.

Now that we have the atomic secret, we must not lose it, and that is what we should risk doing if we should give it to the United Nations or the Soviet Union. But we must make it clear, as quickly as possible, that we are not keeping the bomb a secret for the sake of our power, but in the hope of establishing peace in a World Government, and that we will do our utmost to bring this World Government into being.

I appreciate that there are persons who favor a gradual approach to World Government, even though they approve of it as the ultimate objective. The trouble about taking little steps, one at a time, in the hope of reaching that ultimate goal is that while they are being taken, we continue to keep the bomb secret without making our reason convincing to those who do not have the secret. That of itself creates fear and suspicion, with the consequence that the relations of rival sovereignties deteriorate dangerously. So, while persons who take only a step at a time may think they are approaching world peace, they actually are contributing, by their slow pace, to the coming of war. We have no time to spend in this way. If war is to be averted, it must be done quickly.

We shall not have the secret very long. I know it is argued that no other country has money enough to spend on the development of the atomic bomb, and this fact assures us the secret for a long time. It is a mistake often made in this country to measure things by the amount of money they cost. But other countries which have the materials and the men can apply them to the work of developing atomic power if they care to do so. For men and materials and the decision to use them, and not money, are all that is needed.

I do not consider myself the father of the release of atomic energy. My part in it was quite indirect. I did not, in fact, foresee that it would be released in my time. I believed only that release was theoretically possible. It became practical through the accidental discovery of chain reactions, and this was not something I could have predicted.

I do not believe that a great era of atomic science is to be assured by organizing sciences in the way large corporations are organized. One can organize to apply a discovery already made, but not to make one. Only a free individual can make a discovery. There can be a kind of organiz*ing* by which scientists are assured their freedom and proper conditions of work. Professors of science in American universities, for instance, should be relieved of some of their teaching so as to have time for more research. Can you imagine an organization of scientists making the discoveries of Charles Darwin?

Nor do I believe that the vast private corporations of the United States are suitable to the needs of these times. If a visitor should come to this country from another planet, would he not find it strange that in this country so much power is given to private corporations without their having commensurate responsibility? I say this to stress that the American government must keep the control of atomic energy, not because socialism is necessarily desirable, but because atomic energy was developed by the government, and it would be unthinkable to turn over this property of the people to any individual or group of individuals. As to socialism, unless it is international to the extent of producing a World Government which controls all military power, it might more easily lead to wars than does capitalism, because it represents a still greater concentration of power.

To give any estimate of when atomic energy can be applied to constructive purposes is impossible. What now is known is only how to use a fairly large quantity of uranium. The use of quantities sufficiently small to operate, say, a car or an airplane is as yet impossible. No doubt it will be achieved, but nobody can say when. Nor can one predict when materials more common than uranium can be used to supply atomic energy. Presumably all materials used for this purpose will be among the heavier elements of high atomic weight. Those elements are relatively scarce, because of their lesser stability. Most of these materials may already have disappeared by radioactive disintegration. So, though the release of atomic energy can be, and no doubt will be, a great boon to mankind, that may not be for some time.

Since I do not foresee that atomic energy is to be a great boon for a long time, I have to say that for the present it is a menace. Perhaps it is well that it should be. It may intimidate the human race into bringing order into its international affairs, which, without the pressure of fear, it would not do.

CHAPTER XI

A Myth Exploded

Prime MINISTER ATTLEE's visit to Washington to discuss the atomic bomb has dispelled one illusion; that the United States is the sole possessor of the secret of the bomb. President Truman told his press conference, in mentioning the Attlee visit, that the British and Canadians share the secret, not only the theoretical scientific knowledge, but the engineering know-how. What he did not tell them was that Mr. Attlee was not coming at his special invitation, but at his own suggestion. The President had told Congress he was going to consult the British and Canadians, and then other countries, about the control of atomic energy. But he had taken no step toward consultation, and in the meantime nothing that he said, or that was said officially, suggested anything else than that we have the sole possession of the secret, and are able to share or not to share it as we please. Mr. Truman himself had said we were going to keep it, which indicated that an atomic race with the rest of the world was on. Only when a suggestion came from Mr. Attlee that it was desirable that he visit Washington to discuss the atomic bomb were we brought back to realities. The President then told his press conference that as nearly as he had been able to learn, the entire field of atomic energy release was shared equally by the United States, Great Britain and Canada. A question twice repeated by correspondents in different form as to whether Britain and Canada knew as much about the production of the atomic bomb as we did brought an affirmative answer from the President.

It is, however, difficult to run down the facts about the exact nature of the sharing with the British and Canadians, or what rights they enjoy as partners in the enterprise which produced the bomb. When the atomic bomb was first announced, it was duly stated that its production was a joint enterprise with them. But having been stated, it slipped out of notice, and even out of the minds of some government officials, from the President down. On November 1, 1945, Senator McKellar, president pro tem of the Senate, in proposing that the military use of the atomic bomb be outlawed, also urged that the secret of the bomb be retained by this country. That, he said, was essential if the effort to outlaw the use of the bomb were to succeed. And when Senator Fulbright called his attention to the fact that the British and Canadians know all about the bomb, Senator McKellar replied: "Who knows whether England or Canada knows about it? I do not, and I never heard any evidence to suggest it."

It may be well to go back to Mr. Attlee's announcement of the bomb of August 6, which embodied a private statement about atomic research made to him by Mr. Churchill, which reviewed the British work done prior to 1941. On October 11 of that year, President Roosevelt sent Mr. Churchill a letter suggesting that further atomic work be co-ordinated or even conducted jointly. "Accordingly," Mr. Churchill reported, "all British and American efforts were joined and a number of British scientists concerned proceeded to the United States." By the summer of 1942, this expanded program showed such promising results that the time arrived to build the vast plants for actual production. Britain could not afford interference with its munitions program in the way that building such plants in Britain would have done, and it also was within bombing range of Germany. "The decision was therefore taken," reported Mr. Churchill, "to build the full-scale production plants in America. The main practical effort," he continued, "and virtually the whole of its prodigious cost now fell upon the United States authorities, who were assisted by a number of British scientists. The relationship of the British and American contributions was regulated by discussion between me [that is, Mr. Churchill] and President

Roosevelt, and a combined policy committee was set up. The Canadian government, whose contribution was most valuable," Mr. Churchill said, "provided both indispensable raw material for the project as a whole and necessary facilities for the work of one section of the project which has been carried out in Canada for the three governments in partnership."

Sir James Chadwick was the British scientist heading the British collaborators. Sir James has known the whole story of the making of the bomb. He knows the processes that were employed, the theoretical and engineering problems that were encountered, and how they were solved. In that sense, the British have the secret of the bomb, and all of the secret. If the British cared to spend the necessary money to develop atomic energy on a large scale, Sir James could impart to British engineers the outline of what they need to know to proceed with the design of the installations.

In that sense it is correct to say that the British already have the engineering know-how. But no British engineers took part in the design and construction of the three atomic installations in this country. And British and Canadian partnership presumably does not entitle them to blueprints of the machinery and other equipment used in these installations. The atomic project was for the duration of the war. It was a joint undertaking to serve the common war effort. No doubt the British and Canadians were entitled to atomic bombs, if they could be made and were essential to their war effort. And if the bomb had been completed in February, rather than June, as had been anticipated, it could have been used against Germany. There, you will appreciate, the war effort was a joint one under a combined Allied command, and the question would not have arisen as to whom the bomb belonged. Since the war technically is still in legal existence, the British and Canadians still have a share in the atomic project. They have the same rights as during the war. That, however, is only a technicality, since the British and Canadians have no military need for the bomb.

But you will see that we do not possess the secret exclusively.

All we possess exclusively are the installations. The British and Canadians do not have facilities for making plutonium. Their joint plant in Canada is not on that scale. But insofar as there is any secrecy whatever, the British and Canadians share it fully. And they have just as much to say about what to do with the secret as we have. And that is where the visit of Mr. Attlee takes on importance. He has exercised his rights as atomic partner to come to Washington without waiting for further damage to result from the American policy of secrecy as it has been construed. He has brought our policy back to its original purpose of control and co-operation. It may come as a surprise to many Americans to learn that Mr. Attlee has full rights as a partner. But that is only an instance of the confused and uninformed way the whole matter of the bomb has been treated.

Suggestions in London indicated that Mr. Attlee might propose that the secret of the bomb be placed in possession of the Security Council of the United Nations Organization, and specifically entrusted to the Combined Chiefs of Staff who are to direct the enforcement of the peace for the UNO.

On this subject we have the views of Dr. Vannevar Bush, head of the Office of Scientific Research and Development, credited with being the most trusted adviser of the administration in the field of atomic energy. He wants the United States to share with our world partners all of our basic scientific knowledge of atomic energy. That, he explains, is not sharing the "secret" which he confirms consists only of industrial experience and of the solution of a multitude of practical problems. "No man," he told the Herald Tribune Forum, "could convey this information by a formula or a diagram or two."

But he would have full information as to atomic energy placed in the hands of somebody of the UNO with instructions to disseminate it. "However," he said, "he would do this only if this body has inspection rights, to be implemented by an internationally constituted scientific board. And before the door was opened wide," he said, "he would make very sure that inspection would work." I report this, not because it is sufficient to the need or likely to solve the problem posed by the release of atomic energy. It is important for being the line that may be taken to start with by the British and ourselves.

It may be gathered that Dr. Bush does not consider it enough. For in his speech he declared: "The atomic bomb means that war now would come with volcanic suddenness and volcanic destructiveness to the headquarters of industry and production and could blast the nerve centers of civilization into impotence even before an alert could be spread. The entire pattern in which we are accustomed to think of war is scrapped by this truth. Moreover, non-atomic weapons could by themselves, when fully developed, obliterate civilization. It is therefore imperative for us to prove that the old assumption that wars are inevitable is a fallacy. . . . The self-interest of nations," he said further, "must in the years to come be subordinated in order that the world organization may be strong." And he closed by urging that we remain strong, "and then in this strength lead through the path of international understanding to the organization of a sovereign world."

Dr. Bush did not call attention to the fact, but a sovereign world, one to which the interests of nations are subordinated, is a world government. And if war is to be abolished, it can only be done by establishing a sovereign world. It is not to be done by verbal renunciations as to bombs or war. It also is not to be done by any system of inspection limited simply to physical laboratories, for it is not the atomic bomb alone that threatens civilization; the whole range of aggressive weapons must be controlled. Inspection there must be if war is to be abolished. But that is not to be achieved by inspection alone. It must be inspection with the law behind it, capable of acting against individuals, as the war criminals now are being prosecuted. And to have that, there must be the limitation of sovereignty, and the enforceable law of what Dr. Bush calls the sovereign world.

Dr. Bush may have shied away from the words "world government," but he did not from the idea. And it is to be devoutly hoped his influence with the administration will be to the end that we and the British may take the first steps toward the creation of the sovereign world.

CHAPTER XII

The Military Mind

THE release of atomic energy has engaged, and will continue to engage, three kinds of minds; the scientific mind, the political mind, and the military mind. Each is inclined to be jealous of the other. But none can solve the atomic problem alone. Winston Churchill and Foreign Secretary Bevin, speaking in Parliament in London the week of November 5, 1945, both tried to push aside the scientist as a political power. Mr. Bevin spoke quite solemnly about the very serious claim of scientists to supersede the state. The government, he said, cannot surrender to any section of the community its powers or duties in the field of government. And Mr. Churchill said that whatever is to be decided about atomic energy must be decided by Parliament and responsible government and not by scientists, however eminent and ardent they might be, and he quoted Gladstone to the effect that expert knowledge is limited knowledge.

One can imagine the scientists chuckling over these pompous statements. For they have not asked to supersede the state. All they beg is to be heeded by politicians, to be heard about what atomic power is, and what it is doing to the political structure of society. And in this country they ask to be kept out of any military strait-jacket. As to the quality of the scientific mind, as compared with the political mind, the politicians will be wise not to challenge comparison. The scientists have done wonders, and they have not made anything quite so ugly as the present prospect of peace, which is the product of the unrivalled political and military minds. And if it is argued that the scientists made the atomic bomb, which in turn makes peace so fragile, the scientists can answer that the political and military minds put them to work on that, but that they never made it possible for them to work on releasing atomic energy for peacetime uses.

A quotation from the current Foreign Letter of the Whaley Eaton Service of Washington provides an example of the working of the military mind. It discusses the visit of Prime Minister Attlee. "The great factor most often overlooked," it reports, "is the nature of a nationalistic atomic defense program, which is the necessary alternative to international control of the bomb. War department planners have prepared such a program," the letter states. "It calls, first, for construction and maintenance in a state of permanent wartime alert of a system of rocket and other installations capable of inflicting instantaneous, total destruction on any potentially hostile power; second, for organization of an extensive secret service to give immediate warning of any other power's hostile intentions; third, for the President's 'pressing the button,' which will destroy the potentially hostile power the moment the warning is given. The difficulty is that planners had not completed their plans before they saw that the program was impractical in a democratic society. It would obviously be unconstitutional for a President to press the button for destruction of an ostensibly friendly power without securing a prior declaration of war from Congress—the mere mention of which would cause the potential enemy to press his own button first. It is this which led higher echelons of the General Staff to consider the feasibility of constitutional change."

The letter then goes on to say that because a nationalistic atomic defense policy is neither politically nor constitutionally feasible, there is a natural tendency to give more serious consideration to the alternative of international control! "While it is admitted," it continues, "that international control is at best a dubious experiment, it is argued that it will be better to gamble on a system which has *some* chance of working, than to adopt one known to be unworkable. It is understood that this was Secretary Stimson's view, and before leaving the government he completed a tentative plan for ultimate international control of the bomb. The subject is the most closely guarded in

Washington, but it is believed that Stimson's plan called for creation of an international inspection committee to insure NO manufacture of bombs for purely national purposes, and of a joint British-Russian-French-Chinese-American military body which would control use of the bomb." The letter predicts that Prime Minister Attlee will put forward some such plan, but will wish the control of atomic energy to be a United Nations Organization function. And it remarks that President Truman and Secretary Byrnes will be found ready to be convinced, and that Secretary Patterson, who inherits Stimson's views, will be an ally.

Now that plan to prepare a push-button war to wipe out the whole of any hostile nation is a proper example of the workings of the military mind. And it is characteristic of that mind that, on finding its plan would be unconstitutional, to go on to examine the problem of changing the constitution. Secretary of War Patterson, fortunately, is not equipped with a military mind; indeed one reason for having a civilian at the head of the War Department is to keep the military mind under control. And while this quotation is one of the most extraordinary and dreadful collections of words I have ever encountered, I believe the military mind is altogether correct in its diagnosis of the problem of a nationalist atomic defense. The only way to do it is to wipe out the other nation, and do it first. What kind of world, if any, that would leave is not the concern of the military mind. That is the business of the political thinkers.

Dr. Edward Condon, who has been chosen chief scientific adviser to the Senate Atomic Energy Committee—the McMahon Committee—confirms the concept of a war of the push-buttons, as the result of the release of atomic energy. Writing in the *Army Ordnance Magazine*, he says: "The atomic bombs are such small and simple devices that it is easy to visualize agents of an enemy nation bringing them in in small pieces, under cover of diplomatic immunity, and assembling them quietly in the closets or back rooms of their embassies and consular offices in our chief cities. Then when the decision to make war is reached," he continues, "the ruler of the enemy nation has merely to say the word and his agents in our country can touch off the dozen or two bombs planted in each of our major cities. And within minutes, the entire hearts of each of them are utterly destroyed. Fortunately," he concludes, "there are signs that our political leaders realize the seriousness of the situation and are trying to use it to bring about a world union of peoples and an end to war." It is a comment like this last one—and presumably the proposal of Dr. Einstein for a world government launched by the United States, Great Britain and the Soviet Union—which evoke the censure of the political minds of Mr. Churchill and Mr. Bevin. But it is a misrepresentation of the scientists—at least those in this country—to accuse them of trying to supersede the government, or deprive the politicians of their responsibility. In this country they are doing their utmost to awaken the politicians to their responsibility, not trying to take any of it away. And they are doing this in the first place because they *know* something the politicians only know *about*, the real nature of atomic energy, and the effect it is sure to have on the human race unless prompt and adequate political action is taken.

It is one of the most wholesome developments of this era that nearly all of the scientists who made the atomic bomb are now banded in a body known as the Federation of Atomic Scientists. It represents ninety per cent of the scientists, and they are at the moment dedicated to one or two simple tasks of instruction, and then to opposition to the May-Johnson bill. They want Congressmen to understand that there is no secret of the atomic bomb to be kept, not even a know-how that will keep long; that the two-billion-dollar cost of making the atomic bomb includes three simultaneous approaches toward making it, which no other country need go through, and also the construction of the cities where the experiments were carried through; and finally that there is no specific defense to the bomb. Their logical conclusion is that "in view of the existence of the atomic bomb, no nation can, in this new age, feel secure until the problem of the control of atomic power is solved on the world level."

In their opposition to the May-Johnson bill, they were represented by Dr. H. C. Urey, Nobel prize-winner, who attacked what he called the barbed-wire fence attitude of the Army toward atomic scientists. Scientists talking about the freedom of scientists are, of course, serving their own self-interest, but that does not make it any less the interest of the public. One reason the May-Johnson bill is being pressed by the administration is to hold together the great establishments which are making the bomb and stockpiling plutonium for future use as a source of energy. But the scientists on the projects are hard to keep. And Dr. Urey pointed out that top-flight scientists would not continue to work on such government projects in time of peace, if their freedom of research and free interchange of comment and experience were to be denied them.

"There is no idea of a strike," he explained. "It is the simple fact that one type of scientific employment will look more interesting and attractive than another." But he warned that private enterprise also could not be persuaded to carry on the type of atomic research necessary under the restrictions imposed by the May-Johnson bill.

Some political minds are stretching as the result of the education of the past weeks. One of these is Commander Stassen's. He has not jumped the whole way to the acceptance of the need for world government, but he did come out on November 8 for atomic control on the world level, and advocated outlawing the use of the atomic bomb, save for twenty-five which are to be assigned the United Nations Air Force for the preservation of peace. But if one wants proof that more mind-stretching is needed, take account of the fact that the Administration, the War and Navy Departments and Congress, all of them knowing that we are now in the new era of science in which our very existence hangs by a thread, still have done nothing to get science students out of the draft and out of the armed forces, or to make adequate reparation for the paralysis of science for years ahead decreed by our policy not to make special provision for training scientists during the war.

CHAPTER XIII

The Truman-Attlee-King Conference

THE fruit of the Truman-Attlee-King conference on atomic energy was neither as good nor as bad, neither as constructive and peace-serving, nor anti-Russian and threatening as advance indications had suggested. And it is one of the signs of the confusion in which we live that there should be so much confusion over as straightforward a mission as that of Prime Minister Attlee to Washington to discuss for the first time internationally the impact of the release of atomic energy on human affairs. As I shall show later on, some of the confusion is due to a British mistake in presenting an explanation of Mr. Attlee's purpose. Some of it is due to the seemingly insuperable difficulties these days in getting the airplane of peace to rise from the ground. It is so weighed down by suspicion that nothing that anyone can say or do seems enough to help it into the air. And the one reason there is no war in such a world may be simply because there is no practicable way to fight it. There really is no area of conflict, only misunderstanding and disagreement.

But first let me outline the contents of the joint communiqué on atomic energy released November 15. It starts well. It defines the problem honestly by saying that "the application of recent scientific discoveries to the methods and practice of war has placed at the disposal of mankind means of destruction hitherto unknown, against which there can be no adequate military defense, and in the employment of which no single nation can have the monopoly." This accepts the contention of the scientists that there is no defense against the atomic bomb, and that the secret cannot long be kept. The communiqué goes on to accept the responsibility of the nations which developed the use of atomic energy to take steps to prevent its use for destructive purposes, and to promote its use and the use of other scientific knowledge for peaceful and humanitarian ends.

The communiqué then proceeds to state an important political principle; that the complete protection of the civilized world from the destructive use of scientific knowledge lies in the prevention of war. That, to most students of the problem, is the inescapable diagnosis. Another assertion is then made: that no system of safeguards that can be devised will *of itself* provide an effective guarantee against the production of atomic weapons by a nation bent on aggression, or weapons as threatening to civilization. In other words, no device of controls is enough to assure peace.

If the remainder of the communiqué were as effective as this introduction, it might rank as a great document, and we could do with a great document in this time of crisis. But when the communiqué describes the steps to be taken, these turn out to be startlingly short and timid, in comparison with the stride that science took in releasing atomic energy.

First, there is to be an exchange of fundamental scientific information and the interchange of scientists and scientific literature for peaceful ends with any nation that will fully reciprocate. The results of scientific research are to be made generally available; freedom of investigation and free interchange of ideas are acknowledged to be essential to the development of atomic energy for peaceful purposes. This is good as far as it goes. But the communiqué at once comes to a hurdle—what to do with the industrial know-how. And over this it does not leap. Since the same industrial know-how is needed to make bombs and to use atomic energy for peaceful purposes, there is to be no sharing of the industrial know-how, not until it is possible, the communiqué says: "to devise effective, reciprocal and enforcible safeguards to all nations."

Having stated that *no* system of safeguards will of itself provide an effective guarantee against some nation's making atomic weapons if bent on aggression, this sounds like a contradiction, or at least an undigested inconsistency. And this impression remains on studying the next step proposed. "In order to attain the most effective means of entirely eliminating the use of atomic energy for destructive purposes," a commission is to be set up under the United Nations Organization to prepare recommendations for submission to the organization. This is to be done soon, and the commission is to go to work dealing in separate phases of its task, reporting on each as it completes it. It is to start by working out the details for exchange of scientific knowledge, reporting, to begin with, on an exchange of scientists and scientific information, and then it is to gather full knowledge on natural resources of raw materials.

From there it is to proceed to the problem of control of atomic energy to the extent necessary to insure its use only for peaceful purposes. It goes on to study the elimination from national armaments of atomic weapons and all other major weapons adaptable to mass destruction and finally it studies effective safeguards by way of inspection and other means to protect complying states against the hazards of violations and evasions.

Finally, the communiqué says with truly profound insight: "Faced with the terrible realities of the application of science to destruction, every nation will realize more urgently than before the overwhelming need to maintain the rule of law among nations and to banish the scourge of war from the earth. This," it proceeds, "can only be brought about by giving wholehearted support to the United Nations Organization and by consolidating and extending its authority." But having said that, the communiqué comes to a close on a promise to work for "conditions of mutual trust in which all peoples will be free to devote themselves to the arts of peace."

The good intention is not clinched by the limited program of action suggested. However, it can be said that all that one could hope or pray for does lie in one or two of the phrases of the communiqué. The abolition of war, the extension of the authority of the United Nations Organization in a world of law, the creation of effective safeguards and controls—all these are the elements of a sovereign world, and even if the steps to achieve that world are not proposed, it is something that the American, British and Canadian leaders dimly see the promised land.

Now to take up the misunderstandings about the Attlee plan. One newspaper predicted that the communiqué would be a "virtual ultimatum" to the Soviet Union. And there is a widespread conception that the Attlee plan was deliberately anti-Russian, in that it was not going to share the secret of the bomb until the Russians had formulated their final essential requirements, and these had been found acceptable by us and the British. That happens to be the impression given by a British spokesman who imparted the Attlee plan to Washington correspondents. The impression was unintentionally given. And I am in a position to report what I am assured is the correct version of Mr. Attlee's thinking. He analyzed the present world crisis as being due to suspicions and misunderstandings. We suspect the Russians, they suspect the British and ourselves. They have a right to suspect us because of the way we have been handling the atomic bomb. So, to restore confidence and trust we should prepare to share the atomic secret on a basis of mutual exchange of scientific knowledge. Having done this, it would be legitimate to expect the Russians, for their part, to disarm our suspicions by confiding in us what they really need, if they are to be satisfied in Europe and Asia.

That is the way Mr. Attlee saw things. And stated that way there is no threat or menace or hostility to the Russians in expecting a Russian formulation of minimum requirements. Mr. Attlee actually hoped to rally friendly sentiment to Russia in both America and England, so as to get out of the present tailspin of suspicion. But if it is reported that the Russians are not to have the bomb *until* they come across with acceptable minimum political terms, then his plan does appear as a threat and an act of intimidation. The communiqué itself should undo the damage of the inadequate presentation of Mr. Attlee's views.

But the communiqué is not so convincing as it needs to be,

and it will hardly seem so to the Russians, if only because the industrial know-how of atomic energy is not to be shared until suitable controls have been devised. For the communiqué also says it is not believed that an effective guarantee system can be devised. Now this contradiction may be due simply to the need of drafting a communiqué in which both Mr. Truman and Mr. Attlee could express their views. Mr. Attlee does not believe much in controls. Mr. Truman does. So they both had their say. But the contradiction leaves the communiqué weaker than it really needs to be. For if controls are not possible, why discuss them? And if they are to be sought, why disparage them in advance? Obviously they are to be sought, so it would have been better and far more effective so to announce, without any equivocation whatever.

CHAPTER XIV

Who Are the Realists?

THE British have more reason to fear the atomic bomb than we have, or to put it another way, they already know something about dreadful death that drops down unheralded from the skies. They are geographically in close range of possible rocket sites in any European war. Rockets with atomic explosives are not yet a reality, but they are a definite possibility. Obviously the British Isles are within air range of any possible European belligerent. The small area of Britain, and the concentration of people into cities, make the British more vulnerable to atomic destruction than any other sizable nation. The British do not have the atomic bomb themselves, and though they know all about how to make it, it would cost them heavily to do so. But if they did so, they appreciate that it might work an injury to them rather than give them any added security, for they know that fear is what makes war a danger today. This is the background of the mission of Prime Minister Attlee, and one can see that he came with a greater sense of danger and urgency than fills anyone responsible for American security.

Opinion in Great Britain, however, is divided much as our own is divided. Mr. Churchill is the apostle of secrecy. He is against the bomb, or the know-how, being given to the Russians. Before Mr. Attlee came to this country, Mr. Churchill urged him in Parliament not to press President Truman to share the secret of the bomb with the Russians. To this one can say that Mr. Churchill throughout the war has been an apostle of secrecy, and as highly security-conscious as our highest apostles. It does not necessarily follow that he is too conservative to yield any of British sovereignty, for it was he who offered federal union to the French before their surrender. But it also must be said that Mr. Churchill, in opposing that the secret be shared with the Russians, is not voicing the views of all conservatives. The London *Times,* commenting on the joint communiqué of November 15, questioned the validity of the argument that the know-how of making the bomb is not to be shared until acceptable safeguards have been devised. "This is clearly a case," it said, "where exceptions, once admitted, are apt to create precedents, and end by nullifying the principle at stake. Long-term diplomatic drawbacks of secrecy, in encouraging unwarranted suspicion and mistrust, may well outweigh, on any view of the transaction, such temporary advantages as may be thought to derive from it."

This is an involved way of saying that if you want to create trust, don't start by holding something back. And the *Times* of London must know this has to be said to President Truman, rather than Mr. Attlee, since keeping the industrial know-how is a decision of the Truman administration. It shows how little party lines are indicative, to find the London *Daily Herald,* the Labor organ, arguing that it is justifiable not to share the know-how until operating controls have been set up under the United Nations Organization.

If the communiqué does not pave the road to better relations with the Soviet Union, it goes a long way to meet the demands of unlimited freedom for the scientists. They are to revert to their international status of before the war. Exchanges of scientists and scientific information are to be the first topic on the agenda of the new United Nations commission proposed. And those scientists I have heard speak on the subject have no doubt whatever that the Russian scientists will be just as co-operative as they were before the war. For only in the atmosphere of freedom can Russian scientists, too, function fully and creatively.

The sense of outrage felt by most of the scientists over the proposals of the May-Johnson bill were felt by British scientists over restrictions on them. Professor Marcus Oliphant, one of the leading British atomic scientists, said in a speech that British scientists do not have the guts to make a declaration about the bomb, because they are tied up with the Official Secrets Act, and are afraid that if they open their mouths, they will find themselves in jail. "Perhaps," he said, "I shall find myself in jail before long, but I do feel that these things have to be said as they have been said on the other side of the Atlantic." That is the first intimation we have had that the censorship on the scientists in England has been in any way comparable with that of our own atomic project. Our scientists, since the war, have been free to discuss the political implications of the bomb. But there are important matters about the development of the bomb, not having anything to do with the "industrial know-how" which the scientists still are not permitted to reveal. One of them is the text of the communication made to President Truman after the first experiment at Los Alamos proved to be a success. A number of the nation's foremost atomic scientists addressed to President Truman a plea that the bomb itself should not be dropped over Japan before a test demonstration had been arranged, without loss of life, which would convince the Japanese of our power, and so impel them to end the war. There is no conceivable consideration of genuine security for keeping that document a secret, nor for withholding from the public the reasons which prompted President Truman's advisers to argue the immediate use of the bomb.

One reason suggests itself. We had completed the bomb just in time to use it a week *before* the Russians were due to enter the Japanese war. Had time been taken out to stage the humanitarian demonstration the scientists urged, we should not have been able to, say that the bomb played the part we can now ascribe to it in Japan's surrender. Russia would have won an even greater right to have a voice in Japanese affairs. General Groves still forbids the publication of the appeal, doing so through a provision in the rules of the Manhattan District project that "anything damaging to the prestige of the project," could be suppressed. And evasion of that censorship was punishable by heavy fine and jail sentence, as it still is.

The reason this appeal to President Truman was suppressed appears to have been that it was held to be damaging to the prestige of the project to disclose a difference of opinion within the project itself as to public policy. Obviously, there is no more reason for keeping this appeal secret than anything about Pearl Harbor. It is part of the history of a war, and belongs to the American people.

The scientists are sure to be pleased with the promise of freedom in the joint communiqué, and will applaud it as a good beginning. Almost every scientist of note in this country, signed a draft resolution that does not go much further than the communiqué. It was released November 16, and proposes an immediate conference with the Russians as well as the British, to discuss "the common danger created by atomic weapons." Such a conference, then, would plan for a joint approach to other members of the United Nations Organization to the end of establishing a system of international co-operation and control of atomic energy to prevent a competitive armament race. A great majority of the scientists, I believe, are ready to go much further than this, but this is a statement of virtually unanimous agreement, and so does not go into the problems of sovereignty.

It has been my privilege to meet a good many of the atomic scientists. They are everything they have been cracked up to be; young, fresh, lucid, and fully aware of their social responsibility. Something they seem to fail to make the public appreciate, but which they do communicate in private conversation, is that the atomic bomb is not just another weapon, and that the world has been basically changed by it. The scientists talk much less about the future peacetime uses of atomic energy than laymen. For them it is an instrument of destruction far stronger than people realize. If the public already is in some terror of atomic bombs, it is not in terror enough. And that is said, not to instill panic, but to say that the human crisis is far greater than the response so far made by American people or their government. That is why so many scientists espouse world sovereignty as the essential political solution.

They do this, not because they are idealists, but for the very opposite reason. *They* are the realists, and those who linger with stubborn devotion to sovereignty are the idealists. The scientists know *why* war has to be abolished. Indeed, war, as the old-fashioned folk think of it, already has been abolished. Its place in a world of atomic weapons is taken by universal ruination. I am not able to verify the statement often made that we now have an atomic bomb a thousand times stronger than the one that dropped on Nagasaki. That information is legitimately suppressed. But let me quote the article in the London *Star* of November 15, written by Professor Oliphant, the British scientist. He said that it is possible to produce an atomic poison gas which would kill everything within a thousand miles. "A plant producing nuclear power," he wrote, "produces also a second by-product of the series, radio-active materials. These radio-active by-products are equivalent to thousands of pounds of radium. They could be extracted by an unscrupulous country and sprayed or otherwise distributed over enemy territory in sufficient concentration to prohibit the survival of any living thing. This dissemination of a new type of poison gas, as it were, is free of any difficulties associated with the use of ordinary chemical gases. There is no known method of de-contamination, so that the areas would remain unusable for weeks and months, until radio-activity cleared away." Readers of the Smyth report will recognize that the creation of these radio-active gases is duly recorded in that volume. Professor Oliphant goes on to say: "The only complete solution is offered by a mutual determination of the peace-loving nations of the world to give up completely the use of war." That is the judgment of the realist.

It is not inaccurate to say that the destiny of the human race is now bound up in the outcome of a race between the realists and the idealists. The winning of that race will not be aided by the fact that the idealists are deluded into believing they are the realists and that the realists are the impractical ones.

CHAPTER XV

Facing Facts

I THINK it is well that we should make up our minds that if the world is again involved in a war on a scale comparable with that from which we have just emerged, every weapon will be used. We may confidently expect full-scale atomic warfare which will result in the destruction of great cities, in the death of millions and the setting back of civilization to an unimaginable extent." This is a quotation from Prime Minister Attlee speaking in the House of Common on November 22, 1945. It prompts me to call attention to some of the facts about an atomic war, if it comes, as revealed recently by the scientists who made the bomb. They have made it clear that atomic bombs can be plentiful and that they will not cost exorbitantly. The two billion dollars which were needed for our original atomic bomb project are misleading. All this money was spent, yet only two bombs were used. But that is not to say that each atomic bomb costs a billion dollars. The Manhattan District Project was an experiment that tried three different ways to solve a given scientific problem. It solved it all three of the ways, we are told. But the expenditure on two of the ways will not have to be made another time by any other country. Part of the cost was in erecting a needlessly large industrial plant, but part, too, was to build housing for fifty thousand or more workers in secret communities that had to be thrown up almost overnight.

Dr. J. Robert Oppenheimer, who had charge of the project at Los Alamos, has estimated that the cost of each bomb will be around two million dollars. So for two billion dollars, a government could make a thousand atomic bombs. That is more than enough to wipe out the chief cities and chief industries of any nation on earth if the bombs could be brought to their targets. And if it is only half enough, it will cost only four billion dollars to make twice as many. That is less than two per cent of what this country spent on the war. Atomic warfare might actually turn out to be the cheapest way to fight. Any idea that atomic bombs will be rare, or too expensive for anybody but this country to make is idiotic.

And that brings up the next question, delivering the bombs to their targets. Using them against Japan we needed a base near Japan. But since then a B-29 has flown non-stop from Guam to Washington for the world's long-distance record. Next year we shall have a stronger, larger, longer-ranged plane. So can any other industrial country devoted to the science of flight. German scientists expected to build jet propelled bombers of great speed with a range to attack American cities. Some country can surely have these, if not next year or in the next three or four years, surely by the end of a decade. Then there are rockets, whose range is capable of great expansion, and whose flight probably can be regulated with mathematical accuracy. These are no longer theories or experiments. I shall only mention the stratospheric platforms which General Arnold wrote about in his annual report and which German scientists hold to be well within the range of possibility. Successful atomic war can be waged without reference to anything not already seen by this generation. It will not be necessary to rely on delivering the bombs all the way through the air. They can be sent part way by sea. An improved submarine can bring them to the desired coast, and there launch a plane. Or it can plant a bomb with a time mechanism which will engulf a city under a tidal wave. And finally, there is the possibility of delivering the bomb by secret agents. The bomb itself is small; the explosive part being something that a single person can easily carry. Its exact weight is a military secret, but it cannot be more than twenty-five pounds. True, the presence of a radio-active substance in a quantity great enough to make a bomb would register on instruments already available. But it would take a lot of instruments to make sure that no bombs were being planted and set with time mechanisms in our main cities, or indeed in all of them. It is pointed out that three or four bombs would destroy the city of Washington. If they did, the whole of the government might be wiped out, as probably all political leaders and all members of Congress and the administration would be killed or injured. These possibilities are not the phantasies of a brooding imagination. They are altogether reasonable expectations as to the full-scale atomic warfare which Mr. Attlee said we could confidently expect.

Since we alone possess the bomb at this moment, and it is going to take other countries time to solve the industrial problems of producing it, we do have a little moment in which to adjust ourselves to the reality that others will have it. For it is only a little moment if the whole basis of society has to be given a new foundation, and it must be built in a few years. Building social institutions is normally one of the slowest of operations. The time is short, but not too short. If we are frightened by the potentialities of atomic destruction, and frightened enough by it, we need not be so frightened by the normal slowness of social action. Usually it is foolish to hurry. Now it is foolish not to. It is worse than foolish; it is suicidal.

Everyone who has spoken out about the problem has agreed on the general proposition that there will have to be international control of some kind to prevent the use of atomic power in another great war. Some leave it at that. Some put the proposition more pointedly by saying that there must not be another great war, and that the only certain way to prevent it is to establish a world sovereignty, which transcends national sovereignties, since it is their existence which is the basic cause of wars. Dr. Einstein, as you know, proposed a government of the United States, the Soviet Union and Great Britain, which all other countries would be free to join. More generally, students of the problem want the United Nations Organization used as a starting point, and strengthened until it is vested with the elements of national sovereignty.

In his November 22 speech in the House of Commons, Prime Minister Attlee made a passionate plea for the use of the United Nations Organization. "It is here, it is present in the world," he said. "It was born almost at the same time as the atomic bomb. It is not something vaguely heard of and outside the range of our life. It is fraught with tremendous possibilities. I want everyone in this country, and in the world, to feel their personal concern in the success of the United Nations Organization. Unless we apply to these problems the moral enthusiasm as great as that which the scientists bring to bear on our research work, then our civilization, built up for so many centuries, will surely perish." Mr. Attlee had previously said that through the United Nations Organization, "if all nations resolve to use it, we can establish a rule of law and prevent war." And that obviously is the formula for a world sovereignty to prevent war, something which establishes a rule of law. Mr. Attlee is a socialist, an internationalist, and such ideas are not novel to him.

But let us see what Anthony Eden, the conservative, had to say in the same debate. He agreed with the Prime Minister that no set of rules is going to enable us to survive future wars when this weapon is latent for use, and no safeguards by themselves are going to provide an effective guarantee. "They have got to be accompanied," he said, "by the acceptance of the rule of law among nations. Every succeeding scientific discovery," he continued, "makes greater nonsense of old-time conceptions of sovereignty, yet it is not the least use deluding ourselves. It is true that national sentiment is still as strong as ever. Despite some stirrings the world has not been ready to abandon or modify its old conceptions of sovereignty. Now atomic energy has come to enforce the call for something more. For the life of me," he said, "I am unable to see any final solution that will make the world safe from atomic power other than that we all

abate our present ideas of sovereignty. We have got somehow
to take the sting out of nationalism. We have got to make up
our minds where we want to go. I know where I want to go. I
want to go to a world where relations between nations can be
transformed in a given period of time as the relations between
England, Scotland and Wales have been transformed."

That is a strong plea for world government. But after saying it Mr. Eden proposed the abolition of the veto of the great
powers in the security council of the UNO. His proposal was
echoed in the United States Senate the next day by Senator
Hatch in advocating eventual world government. But one must
be careful not to confuse two separate themes. Abolition of the
veto power can be a mechanism merely enabling certain sovereign
states to outvote another sovereign state. And as the Soviet
Union, and to some extent the United States, fear being outvoted in a world organization by other sovereign states "gang-
ing up" on them with political motives, it does not appear like
the promising way to achieve a genuinely sovereign world.
That might better aim for a central body with full responsibility
for security, having sole possession of atomic and other aggressive weapons, and the power to enforce inspection and control
in the realm of armaments. Even if this sovereignty should
exist, the danger of wars would not have altogether vanished,
for there still might have to be a war of secession before world
sovereignty could be said to be firmly established. Peace, like
liberty, will always cost the price of eternal vigilance. But peace
will be as much easier to obtain in such a world as domestic
security is easier to obtain today than it was in the days of
the robber barons, or the trigger-happy stalwarts on the frontier.

Representative Helen Gahagan Douglas, presenting a resolution in the House, calling for a conference with the Soviet Union
as well as Great Britain on the atomic bomb, rightly said the
real problem is not what to do about the atomic bomb. It is:
Can we live together? "We can afford to split the atom," she
said, "but we cannot afford to split the Big Three. Men must

settle their differences around a council table from here on if man is to have a future. That is what the scientists have been telling us, not because they are suddenly gifted with political foresight, but because daily in their lives they sit down to facts and face them—without prejudice, realistically."

CHAPTER XVI

The Age of the Common Man

THE latter part of November was notable in the domain of ideas for bringing a discussion at the top level of sovereignty. For this is the great discussion which must precede the efforts to abolish war in the atomic age. I am thinking principally of the speech on world government of Foreign Secretary Ernest Bevin in the House of Commons. Strangely enough, that speech was one of the most under-reported of modern times. It seems as if all our newspapers and news agencies in unison slipped up on giving it the space and emphasis it deserved.

I am thinking, too, of the ideas on the other side of the question, such as Senator Connally's remark in the Senate UNO debate that he is not going to run after "some butterfly" of world government. That remark suggests that the mind which made it might be functioning inside a cocoon. "There are some 300,000,-000 persons in India, 400,000,000 in China and 175,000,000 in Russia, who would outnumber us in any world government," said the senator. "I don't want a world government, ever." But since the one sovereignty to be committed to a world government, in the view of the foremost advocates of it today, is in the use of aggressive weapons, which nations are not to be permitted to possess, the only proposal on which the United States could be outvoted would be on questions of making war against some other nation. And to say that, and understand it, makes Senator Connally's objection rather curious. He puts himself in the position of defending the sovereign right of the United States to wage national war. Senator Taylor at once told him that for his part he would rather be outvoted in a world government than have an atomic bomb dropped on him. And if keeping the sovereign right to make war leads nations into an atomic war, the choice is quite fairly stated: be outvoted or be destroyed.

Another American comment on the side of sovereignty was made in a different connection by General Groves, the military commander of the atomic project. He was testifying before the McMahon Committee on the problems of inspection, and according to the New York *Times*, he said inspection would not be foolproof, it would erase national boundaries, it would end the sanctity of the home, and destroy private commercial enterprise. The general also was quoted as saying that he thought that even if 40,000,000 Americans might be wiped out in some future atomic war, surviving Americans would retaliate and could win the war. Here two comments come to mind. The mention of the invasion of the sanctity of the home, if General Groves really made it, is quite delightful, for it evokes a picture of a modern housewife clandestinely at work releasing atomic energy in the kitchen. And as to the imperfections of an inspection system, they hardly seem quite so imperfect as a scheme of living in which 40,000,000 Americans could be wiped out, while surviving Americans still managed to retaliate and win the war. Obviously it is a soldier's business to win a war, even an atomic war, cost what it may. But that is why the professional soldier, as such, is *not* the highest authority in discussing the abolition of war. That is a political problem, a problem for civilians. And as you will see from the quotations I am going to make from the speech of Secretary Bevin, it is his opinion that it is a problem for the common man.

But before quoting his speech, I want to put a relevant question. Has any citizen of an American state, say New York State, lost anything of his sovereignty that is worth keeping, by being a citizen of the United States? Mark you, he is outvoted in our federal union. Quite definitely, he can't make war on his neighbors Pennsylvania or Vermont. But isn't he, in fact, still more sovereign, in being a citizen of the United States than if he were only a citizen of New York? One speaks of "sac-rificing" sovereignty if we enter a world government which alone will have the possession and use of aggressive weapons. But all that has been sacrificed is the sovereign right to wage national war, and if one calls that a sacrifice, with any idea that there is a loss of something valuable, the word is badly used.

Secretary Bevin in his speech objected to another phrase, the *surrender* of sovereignty. "The fact is," he said, "no one ever sur-renders sovereignty. They merge it into a greater sovereignty." Mr. Bevin developed his thinking about world government quite clearly, and it is a line worth following with him. "Law," he said, "must derive its power and observance from a definite source, and in studying this problem I am driven to ask, will law be observed if it is arrived at only by treaty and promises and decisions by governments as at present arranged? In all the years this has broken down so often. I trust it will not break down again, but if it is not to break down again I think it must lead us still further on. In other words, will the people feel that the law is their law, if it is derived and enforced by the adoption of past methods, whether League of Nations, concert of Europe, or anything of that kind? The illustration was drawn of the constitution of the United Kingdom," he said. (That was done by Anthony Eden, who held it up as a model for a world govern-ment.) "Where in the United Kingdom," continued Mr. Bevin, "does the power to make law actually rest? It is not even in this House, it is certainly not in the executive, it is in the votes of the people. They are the sovereign authority."

Mr. Bevin cited the precedent of the creation of the United States out of sovereign, separate states, where the power was made to derive from *all* the people. He recalled Mr. Churchill's offer of common citizenship to France in 1940—at mention of which Mr. Churchill interjected: "We were all in it!" "Often thereafter," Mr. Bevin continued, "I tried to study how we could have given effect to it, and it seemed to me that joint citizenship involved a joint parliament, and joint responsibility. It involved an acceptance of this for certain limited purposes in order to derive the powers of law. I feel we are driven relentlessly along this road: we need a new study for the purpose of creating a world assembly elected directly from the people of the world, as a whole, to whom the governments who form the United Nations are responsible and who, in fact, make the world law which they, the people, will then accept and be morally bound by and be willing to carry out. For it will be from their votes that the power will have been derived, and it will be for their direct representatives to carry it out. You may invent all sorts of devices to decide who the aggressor is, but after all the thought you can give to it, the only repository of faith I have been able to find to determine that, is the common people. There has never been a war yet which, if the facts had been put calmly before the ordinary folk, could not have been prevented. The common man, I think, is the greatest protection against war. The supreme act of government is the horrible duty of deciding matters which affect the life or death of the people. That power rests in this House as far as this country is concerned. I would merge that power into the greater power of a directly elected world assembly, in order that the great repositories of destruction and science, on the one hand, may be their property, against the misuse of which it is their duty to protect us, and, on the other hand, that they may determine in the ordinary sense whether a country is acting as an aggressor or not. I am willing to sit with anybody, of any party, of any nation, to try to devise a franchise or a constitution—just as other great countries have done—for a world assembly with a limited objective, the objective of peace.

"Once we get to that stage," said Mr. Bevin, "I believe we shall have taken a great progressive step. In the meantime, there must be no weakening of the institution which my right honorable friends built in San Francisco. It must be the prelude to further development. This must not be considered a substitute for it, but rather, the completion or a development of it, so that the benefit of the experience and administration derived in that institution may be carried to its final end. For the moment you accept that, one phrase goes, and that is 'international law.' That phrase presupposes conflict between nations. It would be replaced by 'world law,' with a moral world force behind it."

That speech made Mr. Bevin the first Foreign Secretary of a great power—or as far as I know of any nation—to advocate as a practical, attainable objective, the establishment of a limited world government to which is committed the responsibiilty of maintaining the peace. Mr. Bevin did not, as it happens, speak with the full authority of the British cabinet, which has not taken a cabinet decision along the lines he laid out. He spoke personally. But the atomic age has come far and come quickly to have reached this point in the relatively few weeks since the first atomic explosion last July. And Mr. Bevin at once was supported by the spokesman of the opposition, just as he himself had followed the argument for world government made by his predecessor, the Conservative Anthony Eden. So there is harmony at the top political level in Britain, at least, as to the desirability (and the principles) of a limited world government. In British life, it is comparable to a similar statement, if it only had been made, by Secretary Byrnes, seconding a forceful address, if it had only been made, by Governor Dewey.

But if our political leaders have not yet found voices for the proper disposition of national sovereignty, some of our great jurists have. Former Justice Roberts, a Republican, has long been one of the leaders in advocating federal union. In the latter part of November we had a dissertation by Supreme Court Justice William O. Douglas, who declared that all nations must give up part of their sovereignty if international peace is to become a reality. "Problems of defense against aggression can no longer be solved on national lines," he said. "A common defense is essential, and that requires the surrender of some part of sovereignty on the part of all nations. The advent of atomic energy has made plain that self-determination as an absolute principle is not consistent with the requirement of world peace." The justice stressed what needs to be clearly understood, that subject to the requirements of this world government, self-government of all peoples must be the goal. Justice for all people will come from home rule, he said, not from some far away world capital. "The ideal of justice for all people," he said, "has never been achieved by the grace of a ruler supported by an army, it has come only from the people themselves. We must give the peoples that chance, and use our moral leadership to the end that they get that chance." You see, these thinkers agree that the atomic age must be the age of the common man.

CHAPTER XVII

Fear Must Lead to Action

I HAVE been chided by several quite thoughtful correspondents for trying to make people afraid of the atomic bomb. I am told I should not stimulate interest in world government through fear, that people are more likely to respond constructively if approached constructively, and that a moral appeal will assure more desirable reactions than a sense of danger. Fear, however, is part of our stock equipment as human beings. We use it in our everyday life. Under its pressure, we take measures to protect ourselves. Without fear, we should not take the measures. Certainly fear without action is of little use. Fear of unreal things can be destructive. But fear, properly responded to, is quite useful. I am sure the desire to be safe is much stronger than the desire to be good in any particular way. And the moral appeal I am asked to make would have to be aimed at making people good in some particular way. The most impelling argument for world government is not that it will do away with something evil, but that it will do away with something highly dangerous. And the danger from war in the atomic age is so very much greater than it was before last July that it must be explained and expounded, if people are to take the necessary steps for their security. If that invokes fear, it is invoking the standard process of self-protection in the human mind. It seems to me that only those are entitled to object who themselves are fully aware of the increased danger, have done all in their power to make it generally understood, and are conscientiously satisfied that the steps taken to meet it are sufficient.

The atomic scientists find that the lay public thinks of the atomic bomb much as it does of any other weapons. That is why they apply themselves so patiently to the task of public education. Having released atomic energy, and knowing themselves so well what they have done, they cannot rest if they have not made the world aware of it. It isn't that their consciences are uneasy. On the contrary, I heard one of the great scientists ask in a private conversation: "Can you think of any single thing we might have done, better calculated to produce a more beneficial result for the human race?" He was sure the atomic bomb would end war. It would have to end war. But it will do so only if man fears it. We have had the moral reasons for ending war as long as we have had wars. But because war used to be a means of survival, man practiced it. In the atomic age, survival in war is virtually impossible, since atomic destruction can become universal.

In the hearings before the McMahon Committee the first week in December, a hitherto unpublicized scientist, Dr. Philip Morrison, of the Los Alamos Laboratory, scored a great personal success. Senator Johnson called him "the most eloquent witness that I have heard since I have been around Congress. I am sure," he said, "that his power of description must be the envy of all reporters here present. I know it is the envy of all the senators here." Dr. Morrison was sent to the Marianas to assist in the final assembly work on the bombs dropped on Japan. Later he visited the bombed cities. And before the Senate Committee it was his purpose to bring home how different the atomic bomb is from all other bombing operations. He gave a vivid word picture of Tinian, where the B-29's went on their raids over Japan. I wish I could quote all of it; it is a classic of terse description.

"Tinian is a miracle," he said. "Here, 6,000 miles from San Francisco, the United States armed forces have built the largest airport in the world. . . . I have flown many times in a B-29, and I doubt that there is a more complex and wonderful machine of any kind," he continued. "And here, from the factories of Seattle and Wichita, were several hundreds of these million dollar craft. Here were collected tens of thousands of specialists, trained in the operation and repair of the delicate mechanisms which cram the body of the plane. In the harbor every day rode tankers, laden with thousands of tons of aviation gasoline. A net of pipe-lines supplied the air fields with fuel. The radio dial was busy with signals of every kind. And all these gigantic preparations had a grand and terrible outcome." Dr. Morrison described the take-off of these planes, as they left on missions, and then their return. "Most of the planes would return the next morning," he said, "standing in a long single line, like beads on a chain, from just overhead to the horizon. You could see ten or twelve planes at a time, spaced a couple of miles apart. As fast as the near plane could land, another would appear at the edge of the sky. There was always the same number of planes in sight. The empty field would fill up, and in an hour or two, all the planes would have come in. The next day the reconnaissance photographs would come in. They showed a Japanese city, with whole square miles of it wrecked and torn by flame. The fire bombs dropped on wood and paper houses by the thousands of tons, had done their work. A thousand B-29's time and again burned many square miles of a city in a single raid."

Then came the contrast in Dr. Morrison's account of the use of the atomic bomb. "There were," he said, "no shiploads of incendiaries. Instead of all the ordnance men and their bomb dumps, there were about twenty-five people from Los Alamos, a few Quonset huts transformed into testing laboratories and a barricaded building. The strike took off after midnight. The field was deserted. Only two or three planes were warming up. A few lights burned around a single hard-stand. And one plane roared down the runway, took off, and set course for the cities of the enemy. The reconnaissance photos next day told the same story. One plane with one bomb had destroyed many square miles of a city, destroyed them even more thoroughly and with even less chance of resistance or escape than a thousand-plane raid. I can imagine," he said, "a thousand atomic bombs, and an airport like Tinian's to send them off. War can now destroy not cities, but nations.

"There is even more to be said," he continued. "I remember vividly the lunch we had at the prefectural building at Hiroshima. The Japanese officials came there to talk to us, to describe their experiences. I sat at lunch next to the chief medical officer of the district. He had been pinned in the wreckage of his house for several days after the explosion—he lived a little more than a mile from the point of impact—and was still wearing splints. His assistant had been killed, and his assistant's assistant. Of 300 registered physicians, more than 260 were unable to aid the injured. Of 2400 nurses, orderlies and trained first-aid workers, more than 1800 were made casualties in a single instant. It was the same everywhere. There were about thirty-three modern fire stations in Hiroshima. Twenty-six were useless after the blast, and three-quarters of the firemen killed or missing. The military organization was destroyed; the Commanding General and all his staff were killed with some 5,000 soldiers of the garrison of 8,000. Not one hospital in the city was left in condition to shelter patients from the rain. The power and telephone service were both cut over the whole central region of the city. Debris filled the streets, and thousands of fires burned unchecked among the injured and dead."

In describing the bomb, Dr. Morrison said: "When it is detonated in the middle of a city, it is as though a small piece of the sun has been instantly created. There is formed what we have called the ball of fire, which is a hot glowing something about one-third of a mile across, with a temperature of about 4,000,000 degrees Fahrenheit in the center of it. There is a sudden creation and expansion which pushes away, with terrible violence, the air that once occupied this region. This air, shocked into motion, moves just like a blast wave from a great explosion of TNT. This pushing air creates an enormous pressure, even a great distance away. Behind the waves of pressure, there come great winds, 500 to 1000 miles per hour, winds which damage and destroy all structures."

He then described some of the effects. "If you are near the sun," he said, "you must expect to get burned. The people near it are burned on the body, the people and the structures underwent terrific radiant heat. Instantly all organic material was burned up, over some distance it burned the flesh. There are two more effects. At the instant of the explosion there are emitted from this small sun not only the great push through the air, the violent blast, there is not only the concentrated heat, there was also a great amount of radiation, like the radiation used by doctors, X-ray radiation used for the treatment of cancer. This radiation was very penetrating. There is no protection behind a foot of concrete, for example. Of those persons within a thousand yards of a blast, one in every house or two—about five or ten per cent—escaped death from blast or from burn. Many crawled out of the wreck of their homes relatively uninjured. But they died anyway. They died from the effects of radium-like rays emitted in great numbers from the bomb at the instant of explosion. This radiation affects the blood-forming tissues in the bone marrow, and the whole function of the blood is impaired. The blood does not coagulate, but oozes in many spots through the unbroken skin, and internally seeps into the cavities of the body." Dr. Morrison concluded: "It goes without saying that, like most of the scientists of the project, I am completely convinced that another war cannot be allowed."

I have only given selections from Dr. Morrison's remarkable testimony. But it should be enough to demonstrate that the atomic bomb—and it already is far more powerful than the one that hit Hiroshima—is worth fearing, if the fear is the kind which induces action. For us all, self-preservation is at stake.

CHAPTER XVIII

Dr. Szilard's Testimony

THE name of Dr. Einstein has been most prominently associated, in the minds of the public, with the initiative that interested President Roosevelt in the possibility of making the atomic bomb. But while Dr. Einstein wrote the letter which Alexander Sachs laid before the President in October, 1939, it was the work of two scientists, Fermi and Szilard, to which he called President Roosevelt's attention. "Some recent work of E. Fermi and L. Szilard," his letter said, "which has been communicated to me in manuscript, leads me to expect that the element uranium may be turned into a new and important source of energy in the immediate future." And along with this letter was a memorandum by Dr. Szilard, making specific predictions about the possibility of using atomic energy to make a bomb of a power beyond all military conceptions.

During the week of December 14, the Senate Atomic Energy Committee made the acquaintance of Dr. Szilard in person, and the newspaper readers of the country would have come to know him better, if the Committee hearings had not been competing with the Pearl Harbor and General Hurley hearings, not to mention labor troubles. By any true news values, Dr. Szilard is worth knowing well, and his testimony proved to be thought-provoking to a degree unusual even in the experience of this committee. Like others of the great scientists, he has the most concise way of saying something profound, as for instance, his statement that we fear the Soviet Union not because *it* has the atomic bomb, but because *we* have it.

Dr. Szilard, in February, 1940, wrote a paper stating that a chain reaction can be maintained in a mass composed of graphite and uranium. The Germans did not learn of this fact because the statement, though sent to the *Physical Review,* was submitted with the request that it be withheld from publication. Dr. Szilard was already all for keeping atomic secrets from the Germans by voluntary action. But as a Senate witness, he sharply criticized the system of compartmentalization—the secrecy device used on the official atomic project. This kept a scientist in one department from knowing what a scientist in another department was doing. This is not the most important part of Dr. Szilard's testimony, and I mention it first because of the estimate he made that the United States might have had the atomic bomb eighteen months earlier—in the spring of 1944—if this system of secrecy had not been in force. It was not the Army which first applied it. It was introduced before General Groves took it over, by the commission headed by Dr. Bush and President Conant, and it may help explain why some of the scientists regard these eminent colleagues as having gone brass-hattish. General Groves, however, applied it with the best of Army zeal, and the secrecy maintained on the project is the pride of the Army. Had the bomb been ready in the Spring of 1944, it might have made an incalculable difference to the history of the war, and indeed of the human race. Perhaps it is just as well that it wasn't used. Be that as it may, it is hardly an argument for compartmentalization. Dr. Szilard testified that the scientists got as far as they did and as quickly as they did by breaking the rules. They told each other secretly what they were doing, and in this way found what information was available, which they then could ask for in the routine way. For there was a department to which they were entitled to go for such information. The trouble was that without freedom of exchange they didn't know what to ask for. If we had not had compartmentalization, we might have learned by the fall of 1940 that a bomb could be made from light uranium. As it happened, the British, who did not use this system of secrecy, put two and two together and found it out. And they told us about it. And that enabled us to get along as quickly as we did. But if we had found it earlier by ourselves, the bomb might have been ready for use well before the invasion of Normandy.

Members of the Senate Committee tried to argue with Dr. Szilard that our secrecy system is vindicated by the fact that the Germans had no idea whatever that we were making an atomic bomb. But Dr. Szilard pointed out that the Germans had no idea that any of our great installations even existed, those at Oak Ridge, on the Columbia River, in Chicago, and in New Mexico. And that was not due to the knowledge being compartmentalized. It was simply poor espionage work by the Germans. As it turned out, compartmentalization didn't affect the Germans in any way. It simply hampered our scientists.

I should report that Dr. Szilard did not argue to the committee the utter necessity of world government. He proposed instead the abolition of the manufacture of stockpiles of material for the bomb, for a period of years. He said it would be easier to control a complete ban on the use of atomic energy, than to control its *misuse*. He would have the ban arrived at by agreement which any party to the agreement could legally abrogate. Then, if abrogated, some time would be needed before bombs could be made, or indeed any fissionable material. That would be time in which some preparation for war could be made, and some dispersal of industry would be possible. If any nation served notice that it was ending an agreement not to use atomic energy, that obviously might lead immediately to a preventive war, but it would be a war without atomic bombs at its outset, at any rate.

The plan is interesting for showing that this alternative to world government is anything but impressively secure as a system. I imagine that Dr. Szilard would agree, but he might argue pessimistically that there is no hope at this moment of inducing the Soviet Union *or* the United States government to merge their sovereignties into a world sovereignty, and that this is the best that can be done for the present. Dr. Szilard, however, did not argue that we have a head start on the Russians, or that the secret of the know-how gives us any margin of safety. On the contrary, he was emphatic about it that plutonium—one of the fissionable materials from which the bomb can be made—can quite easily be manufactured by any other industrial country. "As far as the production of plutonium is concerned," he declared, "any competent mechanical or chemical engineer who spends some time thinking about the problem can see that no precision work is involved in the manufacture of plutonium." The design which we actually used did, he said, "require somewhat narrow tolerances and high-class workmanship, which we could afford, because we have this workmanship in abundance. . . . Naturally," he continued, "a country like Russia need not choose just this kind of design, but might prefer a design which does not require high precision work. The statement has been made before this committee," he went on, "that it requires high precision work such as can be provided by only a few countries, including Switzerland, to make atomic bombs. As far as the production of plutonium is concerned, such a statement would have no basis in fact." He went on to say that he saw no reason why any country that is capable of industrial development should not be able to build plutonium factories. True, it would have to have the uranium, and the question, so far as Russia is concerned, is whether it has available uranium ores. But he said he thought it exceedingly foolhardy to assume that in the vast territory of Russia no adequate deposits of low-grade ores could be found if prospecting were carried on in earnest.

Dr. Szilard gave the Committee a clear understanding of the difference economically in the use of light uranium and plutonium. Light uranium, or uranium 235, is extracted by a laborious process from natural uranium, and it accounts for less than one per cent of the natural uranium, so its quantity is limited by the amount of natural uranium available. Before the war, we imported 400 tons of uranium a year, and from this we would do well to extract two tons of light uranium. If we "burned" this—that is, used it by allowing it to disintegrate—and used the heat it generated to make steam, and the steam for the production of electricity, we should have a million and a quarter kilowatts, or about as much as the average production rate of TVA in 1944.

But plutonium can be made in much larger quantities. "Plutonium," Dr. Szilard explained, "can be manufactured from a component of natural uranium which accounts, not for one per cent, but for more than ninety-nine per cent of the natural uranium." We can use heat in two ways from plutonium. It is generated in the process of making plutonium, and then again when the plutonium is "burned." The amount of plutonium, if it is stored, can increase almost geometrically. "For instance," said Dr. Szilard, "if you start with one ton of production in 1946, you might produce two tons in 1947, four tons in 1948, eight tons in 1949, and sixteen tons in 1950." But assuming that the quantity could not be made to increase at such a rate, and it took three years to double it, we should have sixteen tons of plutonium by 1958. And in fifteen years we should easily have twenty tons, which then could be "burned." And this amount would produce electrical power at a rate of about 15,000,000 kilowatts. That is more than ten times the power now produced by TVA. Or, to quote Dr. Szilard, "the amount that would be produced by burning twenty tons is equal to the total electrical power production produced by utilities in the United States before the war." And the twenty tons are by no means an upper limit. "We might," he said, "produce very much larger quantities if we can find customers for the electrical power produced."

Asked about the relative cost of atomically produced electrical power, and the power now in use, Dr. Szilard had to put up his warning finger. That is secret information, and he could only give it in executive session. But he said: "Clearly I would not talk about it, if I did not think it possible that ten years from now it will be much cheaper, that uranium as a fuel will be much cheaper than coal."

But we are not to have this vast reservoir of energy if Dr. Szilard's pessimistic political view is right. We would forego the peacetime use of atomic energy, because we could not be sure not to go to war with atomic bombs. Maybe the world *is* so benighted. Would it not be saner, however, to assume that people *can* take the wise way and prevent war altogether?

CHAPTER XIX

We Must Abolish War Itself

W HEN historians come to review these times, they will do so partly in terms of the release of atomic energy, and events in reaction to it. The week of December 21 produced two reactions of note. One is the first discussion between ourselves and the British on the one hand, and the Russians on the other, about the future control of atomic energy. That discussion was held in Moscow.

One reason Secretary Byrnes proposed going to Moscow was to hold this discussion. He did not do this out of a sudden impulse. From the time the bomb was first used it was recognized as an international problem. Since it had been developed by the British and Canadians as partners in the project, they had particularly keen interest in the international problem presented by the bomb. It was in September that Prime Minister Attlee proposed a personal discussion with President Truman. And in his message to Congress on October 3, the President made known his intention of discussing, first with Britain and Canada, and then with other nations, the conditions under which co-operation might replace rivalry in the field of atomic power. Later, in his Navy Day speech, the President stated that discussion of the atomic bomb with Britain and Canada, and later with other nations, could not wait upon formal organization of the United Nations. The talk with Britain and Canada was duly held.

The talk with "other nations" has now carried the statesmen logically to Moscow. It was being held, as the President said it must be, before the Assembly meeting of the United Nations, scheduled for January 10. Obviously there will be little possibility of replacing rivalry with co-operation in the field of atomic energy if the Soviet Union does not join with us, the British and Canadians in planning the nature of that co-operation. We in this country have been dangerously obscure as to our intentions along these lines. The emphasis on the bomb's being a secret—which President Truman himself once placed there— has not inclined the Russians to consider us as dedicated to friendliness and headed for peaceful co-operation. They regarded the bomb as part of our arsenal of power—and so did we. Hence they have believed it to be a factor in our conduct in international relations. Historians are pretty sure to record as one of the baffling blunders of our statesmanship that we permitted the atomic bomb to engender the fear it has created. But they will also record that this has not been our real intent. We want to make a world of peace, and were misled into acting as though we could do it by creating fear. Now we are acting to create confidence. We have gone to Moscow, have laid at least some of the cards on the table face up, and are asking the Russians to join with us in setting up a commission under the United Nations which is to study the problem of the exchange of scientific information and the control of the use of atomic energy.

The Russians are not being given what is called the "know-how" of making the bomb, but it is stupid to lay much stress on whether to give or keep this knowledge from them, since they are sure to come by it through their own efforts. It was made clear, in the procedure adopted in the conference President Truman held with Prime Ministers Attlee and Mackenzie King, that full exchange is not to be arranged with other nations until it is reciprocal, and until the problem of control has been studied. Whether historians will judge that we have done enough to create confidence in Moscow is another matter. But now a hand has gone out to the Russians in which there is no bomb, visible or invisible, and that undoubtedly is the present top-ranking news in the world of reality.

Ranking second, I should put the speech of Prime Minister

Mackenzie King in the Canadian Parliament. Once again a vital speech has not received anything like the space it deserves in our newspapers. Foreign Secretary Bevin was the first foreign minister to come out frankly for the merger of sovereignties into a world sovereignty for the maintenance of peace. Mr. Mackenzie King will have the fame in history of having been the first Prime Minister to have done so, in a speech which was even more specific than Mr. Bevin's.

One may well ask why it should be that we cannot have as good speeches from President Truman and Secretary Byrnes. If ever a domain should be claimed by Americans, it is the domain of service in the cause of peace. Any statesman who speaks out with conviction and faith for an organization of world society that can abolish war can bank on the wholehearted support of the American people. If we took our world leadership seriously, we would not yield in initiative and vision to any other nation.

We can be grateful to Mr. Mackenzie King for giving us a better view than we have had of the conference he attended in Washington. "At Washington," he said, "we were called upon to consider not merely the elimination of the atomic bomb, but also the kind of world order which is necessary in an atomic age, if civilization is to survive. We were seeking to take the first step in an effort to rescue the world from a desperate race in weapons of mass destruction. At the same time we sought to make very clear that the responsibility for devising means to insure that the new discovery—the release of atomic energy—should be used for the benefit of mankind, instead of as a means of destruction, rested not on our nations alone, but on the whole civilized world." But Mr. Mackenzie King made it clear that the atomic bomb is only part of the problem. "Nothing can be more true," he said, "than that without unremitting co-operation and the united effort of nations, there will be no enduring and effective protection against the atomic bomb, as well as against the indiscriminate use of poison gas or the latest refinements in gas warfare, and against bacteriological warfare, all of which are even more frightful methods of human destruction than the atomic bomb. To insure civilization from destruction, it is not enough to banish atomic, or gas, or bacteriological warfare. We must abolish war itself."

It was on the subject of control that the Canadian Prime Minister was most explicit. In the atomic era, he said, the problems are primarily political, the problems of relations between men and governments. "Fundamentally," he said, "they are part of the age-old conflict between good and evil. As such their ultimate solution will be found only in the realm of philosophy and morals. One thing is certain," he declared, "they admit of no mechanistic solution. By themselves, devices for the control of atomic energy are at best but temporary expedients. For this reason, I believe, it is an error to contemplate the control of the use of atomic energy in commodity and police terms, as if atomic energy were some new and dangerous drug. Technical scientific controls of production, processing, and final disposition are indispensable, but they are obviously inadequate. It would, I believe, be criminal folly to allow ourselves to imagine that the peace and security of mankind can be attained by any scheme of commodity control. The more deeply one ponders the problems in the light"—the terrible light, as Mr. Attlee said—"of the implications of the development of atomic energy, the harder it is to see a solution on anything short of some surrender of national sovereignty, with a limited surrender, at least at the outset, to matters pertaining to the prevention of war and the maintenance of international security.

"The United Nations Organization," the Canadian Prime Minister continued, "is not a sufficient answer to the problems of peace and security which the world is now seeking. It is a first step, and an all-important step, in the direction of that co-operation between nations which is essential to the survival of civilization. It is not the only, much less the final, step. The United Nations Organization is an indispensable medium and channel and forum through which the peoples of the world can work out new institutions and arrangements which their peace

and security now require. If we are agreed on the ultimate
necessity of some measure of world government to maintain
world security, we should, by every means in our power, support and strengthen every agency of international co-operation
and understanding which can help to make the world community
a reality. Humanity is one. We must act in the belief that no
nation and no individual liveth to himself alone, and that all are
members one of another."

There are men in Washington who will scoff at Mr. Mackenzie King, saying he is not talking realistically. There are
men who are willing to talk like Mr. Mackenzie King, but only
in private, because they deem it not yet opportune to do so in
public. Either they are poor judges of what is opportune, or the
Canadian Parliament and public are much more modern than
our own.

Senator McMahon's Atomic Energy Committee is the one
organ of government in this country studying all aspects of the
atomic bomb. Once again its hearings have had to compete with
the Pearl Harbor hearings for newspaper space. The Senator
remarked to the National Liaison Committee on Atomic Information that after an atomic Pearl Harbor, there won't be enough
statesmen left for a coroner's jury. "People," he said, "must be
made to understand the gravity and urgency of this problem.
Talk of taking action and working toward a solution over the
next twenty years is dangerous." The senator also applied another word to it: "It is unrealistic. The best guess of the experts," he continued, "is that we have three to five years in
which to choose peace or world destruction. Some say we must
make haste slowly and move by stages. The bomb, however,
won't go off by stages. It is not enough to do one thing, wait
and see if the temperature remains normal, and then do the next
thing." The McMahon Committee has been receiving an education on atomic energy, and Senator McMahon realizes that the
public too must get the same education. "It must," he declared,
"learn the facts so that it will be ready to take heroic decisions."

CHAPTER XX

There Is a Mechanism

CHRISTMAS, 1944, when there was no peace, peace was what we longed for. This Christmas we have the peace. For most Americans this Christmas was a happy one, in the simplest terms of reunion, and the knowledge that a great danger had passed without cutting us off from those we love. But I believe it is true that for most of us, even if it was a happy Christmas, it was also an uneasy one. There is peace on earth, but there is not the good will among men which is the test and proof of it. We realize that the peace we enjoy is the absence of war, rather than the presence of confidence, understanding and generous conduct. We are not children; we know that peace is something that has to be won, it does not flower like a miracle at the end of a war. We know we have not won it yet. And many are dispirited because they do not see how it is to be won, the political constellations being what they are, both abroad and at home.

One kind of letter comes to me more often from listeners than any other, one which asks, almost in prayer: What can I *do*? An obvious answer to such a cry is to say: Be patient. For it is not true that individuals no longer count, and do not have a share in creating events. True, there is little time for patience, perhaps less than there ever has been before, in a tide of crisis. But individuals can think and feel. And in this country, thought and feeling can and do mount quickly to action, and action to change and change to reform. Probably individuals never lived in a time when they could be surer than now of counting. Look back ten years, or only five years, and measure how much each of us has changed his thinking, his feeling, and his understanding of the nature of peace. As a nation, we have taken huge, almost incredible strides. We have emerged from isolation. And we *believed* in isolation, in its being a virtue, a really decent way to live, because we were minding our own business and not out to take anything from anybody in a sordid world. Now we are the world's leading nation, not only its best-off and most productive, but its leading nation. It is a long, long way from isolation to leadership. We have gone this vast distance in five years. And we have done so because individuals have made their contribution to their times. They made a gift. It was first of all a gift of being, which came before any gift of doing. It was a gift of each being a world citizen. I am not saying that we are ripe and wise world citizens. But we have surged forward into world citizenship with wonderful swiftness.

Now individuals can make another contribution, another gift of being. They can *be* persons of peace. They can cultivate good will. Above all, they can think about peace and how it is brought to pass. For there is in democracy what, in olden times, was called a mystery. It isn't really mysterious, it is simply obscure and unobvious. It is this: that when enough individuals, each as a separate entity and an original source of thought and feeling, concentrate on something, their emotion produces action, and change and reform follow. This happens visibly in an election when men and women go to the polls. But it also happens invisibly—without any voting. It happened, for instance, without an election before the adoption of lend-lease. It happened again in the year or two before the election of 1944, when the American people decided that henceforth this nation must bear its share of the responsibility for peace.

There is a mechanism in a democracy which operates in the free flow of thought and expression. One can point to newspaper editorials, and platform speeches, and magazine articles. But it is not these which constitute the change. They only accompany it. The change is something streaming forth from vast numbers of individuals, of which there is no record and, if

you please, no scientific proof. But it works wonders. If five
years ago, anyone would have told you that by now Congress
would have voted this country into a world organization of
collective security, and done so overwhelmingly, without fili-
buster, or long and bitter debate, you would have shaken your
head. Now it has happened, but not because men in Congress
changed their minds, though they did. It happened because tens
of millions of American individuals took up the question of
peace, did so earnestly, and individually; and each came to a
kind of conclusion about it.

Mind you, they did not come to the same conclusion, or a
final conclusion. Some favored a new league of nations. Others
were ready to go into a world federation. Those ready for a
world federation were not all in favor of the same kind of
federation. Some followed Clarence Streit in aspiring to a union
of the democracies. Some followed Robert Lee Humber in
wanting a broad world federation based on law.

The great discussion about the nature of peace held in this
country in the last few years is, I am sure, the greatest ever held
in any land, on any theme, in the history of man. There never
has been such a debate. It reached out from the cities to the
towns, from towns to the villages and hamlets and on to the
farms. We think of the American Revolution as having been a
great decision of the people on this continent. But not a fraction
of the people heard or talked about relations with England in
the 1770's that have talked in our time about the nature of peace.
During World War I, even though it produced unprecedented
paroxysms, only a minority of Americans can be said to have
come to grips with world problems and reached an individual
judgment. But World War II was more nearly total war, and
because of this, and because of improved communications, far
more could take part in both the danger and the thinking of
wartime. In this country, where the danger was least, there was
no less thinking, there undoubtedly was more. And the people
having thought about it, the obscure mechanism of democracy
could start functioning. One saw it when the Republicans

adopted the Mackinack resolution. One saw it in the campaign of 1944, and later in the adoption of the UNO charter. As a nation, we put isolation behind us. The cause for which Woodrow Wilson fought and died, triumphed.

That being true, why should we feel uneasy? Haven't we won the peace in thinking through what its nature is? Why can the peace of today be called no more than the cessation of war? The answer is that we haven't finished thinking through the nature of the peace. We have done two things, accepted our responsibility for the peace, which is what matters most. And we have also designed a world organization. It is the design which is incomplete. For it is a design for a world which, if it ever fought again, would wage war as World War I and World War II were waged. It would be total war, but it would not be total annihilation. At the time the design was made, it did not satisfy those who recognized that to have lasting peace, one must abolish war. More people, I think, were ready at the time of the San Francisco conference for a world federation than our politicians have any idea of. They had been drilled in the logic that there must be a law above nations, if an end is to be put to the anarchy of war. But these people probably were in a minority at that time, though not as small a minority as the so-called "practical" folks thought. I believe that people began to be uneasy while the San Francisco conference was going on. There were conflicts in the air which boded no good. The charter seemed inadequate. And looking ahead, one could see that a development of rocket weapons and air power and electronics was going to make the next war something utterly different from the last two. Besides, collective security in a world of three powers was far less trustworthy than it would have been in the eight-power system in Woodrow Wilson's time. As I said, people began to feel uneasy during and after San Francisco, before the atomic bomb was heard of. And then that burst, and the problem of the peace was utterly changed.

Now the alternative to peace is not war. It is annihilation. Now peace, at whatever spiritual effort, at whatever ethical price, is the most practical proposition we shall ever have to deal with. Nothing can be called more impractical than to be destroyed. All of man's conservatism is now evoked. If we are to conserve, if we are to spare and save, we must abolish war. Those who say to you, we must merge national sovereignty into a world sovereignty, at least for the control of aggressive weapons and the means to wage war, are not the radicals. They are the practical men and women of our time. They are the conservatives. Those who dally with old ideas of sovereignty are wild-eyed radicals. They are willing to risk everything, your life, your nation, your very physical existence, to hold to their obstinate and obsolete ideas of a social order. They are not evil, these men, they are not even wrong. They are just irrational. They have not understood the meaning of the release of atomic energy. They do not get it into their minds that the greatest single social change in the history of the human race has begun before their blurred eyes. They can't be blamed for it. But they forfeit their leadership to the guidance of the minds of individuals in the mass, to the American people. If ever in our history the American people must be relied on to do the brave and wise thing, it is now. And if we are uneasy, it is because we know our task is not completed. May we continue to feel uneasy till it gets done.

CHAPTER XXI

The Moscow Conference

IT WOULD be absurd to undervalue the success at Moscow in assuring a start toward the international control of atomic energy. But it would be folly to exaggerate it. Had the Soviet Union not acquiesced in the procedure proposed by this country, Britain and Canada under the United Nations Organization, we should have been on notice that catastrophe is unavoidable. The armament race would have been on, not only the unacknowledged race which we started by making bombs after the end of the war and announcing that we were going to keep the secret, but on, formally. And thereafter all that the nations did together would be the doom of failure, for we should know that the main door of co-operation had been slammed shut, bolted and padlocked. That has been avoided, and avoiding it has been the measure of the success in respect to atomic energy in Moscow.

But the main door of co-operation has not been opened. All that has been achieved is that a procedure has been accepted which in time may lead to its being opened. A commission is to be set up by the Assembly of the United Nations. It is to go through the stages outlined at the Truman-Attlee-Mackenzie King conference. It will start working out a series of proposals. Four stages are foreseen. First will come proposals for exchange of basic scientific information for peaceful ends. Then will come proposals for controlling atomic energy to the extent necessary to insure its use only for peaceful purposes. Then are to follow proposals for the elimination of atomic weapons and other major weapons of mass destruction from national armaments.

And only at the end of these three steps will proposals be drafted for safeguards by inspection and other means to protect complying states against violations and evasions. So there will be no inspection system controlling atomic energy until atomic weapons and all other weapons of mass destruction have been eliminated from national armaments.

Judging from the failure of sovereign nations to reduce armaments under the League of Nations, plenty of trouble lies ahead. An immediate, formal armament race has been avoided at Moscow, but its place has been taken by an obstacle race. It is even worse, for the obstacles are not the kind that skill and training fit anyone to leap over. A task is being undertaken by sovereign nations which to be achieved must limit sovereignty. And nothing was said about that at Moscow. Nor will it be said by Secretary Byrnes, nor by the Senate Foreign Relations Committee as now constituted, nor even by President Truman. Nor, to be precise, will anything be said by the Russians. All that can be expected in the way of public utterance must come from the British and Canadians; that is, until American public opinion makes itself felt.

So the news from Moscow is a challenge, not an invitation to relax. Some time has been won, and not much more. The problem of atomic energy has not been solved; what is worse, it has not been faced.

To support a sweeping statement like that, let me quote to you an analysis of atomic problems adopted by the faculty of Colgate University. "It is strange," its report says, "that the greatest of all physical discoveries since fire should, in the twentieth century, force a momentous choice between good and evil; and the crisis," it continues, "is fraught with tragic possibilities because there is much in human nature and institutions to make it uncertain that the right choice will be made. It is at least conceivable that the use of atomic energy will result in universal disaster."

The report recognizes that atomic energy is not in itself a problem, but an opportunity, offering the hope that man can throw off his shoulders many of the burdens he has always borne. "With it, perhaps," it says, "it will be possible to diminish the inequality caused by differences in the natural resources of countries and regions, and make many of the historic causes of war obsolete; to revolutionize the world's productive processes; and to cure at least some of the diseases of the human body."

The problem, say the Colgate professors, is not atomic energy, but the bomb. And it now becomes our heavy responsibility as the first makers and first users of atomic energy to lead the world in splitting the atom for life, not death. The report then presents two alternatives. We can assume that world war within the next two or three decades is a probability. Or we can assume that there must be no future war. It points out that the two assumptions are mutually exclusive. There is no practicable middle course. And it then outlines what we must do if we accept either of the assumptions.

If we believe there is to be war within two or three decades, the United States, it says, "should embark on a large-scale program, under closely guarded secrecy, of scientific research and technological development to produce weapons as potent as possible. The United States government," the report proceeds, "should suppress the free exchange of scientific information, both nationally and internationally. It should make plans and start construction for dispersing industries from present centers and build key facilities and living quarters underground, not only for technical staffs and military forces, but for a large percentage of our population. It should maintain large professional armed services and install universal military peacetime training. It should apply totalitarian controls over our entire economy and restrict civil rights in order to safeguard against sabotage. It should be constantly ready to wage preventive war without regard to democratic procedures. It should reduce the standard of peacetime living and the standard of all but technical education, and increase taxes and public debt to pay the cost of the whole program. Underlying all this activity should be the grim recognition that in atomic war the United States would possibly be the first and most vulnerable target."

That is the first assumption, and don't think it is a hobgoblin sketched on the wall to frighten innocent people. There is not a proposal in this part of the analysis for which a hard-bitten advocate is not to be found in Washington. It is obvious that our defense system is bound to be run on the assumption that war is possible. The Colgate professors in looking down the vista of war see precisely what the generals see who have to prepare for that war. The difference between them is that the Colgate professors have put it down on paper, which would be fatal for a general to do. And there is the all-important difference that the professors set down the alternative, and wholeheartedly accept it. They adopt the assumption that there must be no future war.

"Acting on this assumption, and acknowledging that only by multilateral acceptance of the rule of law under responsible world authority can peace be maintained, the United States," the report says, "should rise to its opportunity for constructive leadership. As the present sole possessor of the atomic bomb, the United States should take the first steps to dissipate the atmosphere of mutual misunderstanding, suspicion and fear in which war is nourished. A number of steps," it says, "can and should be taken *now*." We should immediately announce that we have stopped making the atomic bomb, pending an international conference. "Since the United States and the Soviet Union have emerged from World War II as the chief powers, and their mutual fears and contrasting political systems constitute the greatest source of danger, the United States should," it is stated, "conspicuously invite the USSR, along with other nations, to *propose* plans for preventing the use of atomic bombs by any power, a world government included." We should offer to share on a reciprocal basis the fruit of our research in atomic energy, and all other fields, with all other nations, to encourage the widest peaceful application of human knowledge. Being already on record against the use of force in international relations, we should implement our declaration by proposing progressive, multilateral reduction in armaments, military training, and military bases, to the minimum required for police protection under the UNO or under a future world authority responsible to all peoples.

"The United States," the report says, "should state clearly the *extent* to which it is prepared to modify its conception of complete national sovereignty, in order to implement policies and actions that would strengthen the United Nations Organization. It should use its influence to prepare colonial peoples for eventual self-government. It should review national policies with an eye to removing economic conflicts, racial prejudices and other underlying causes of war."

The professors then make one of their sagest observations. "World co-operation," they say, "depends in the long run on the information, ideas and attitudes of *individual* men everywhere. The United States," they proceed, "should invite other nations to join with it in a crusade of education, domestic and international, and on all levels, through schools, colleges, churches, adult education and publicity channels. The purpose should be to promote mutual understanding and friendship among peoples; to persuade men that despite differences of beliefs and institutions they can be united through the awareness of common frailties and aspirations; to insist that the discipline of the emotions in the exercise of moral choice is an inescapable human responsibility; and to demonstrate that in an atomic age the making of a co-operative and peaceful world is not merely moral idealism: it is practical politics and essential for survival. In this, as in all other proposals of this alternative, the facilities set up by the United Nations Organization should be used and strengthened."

What has taken place at Moscow should be examined against the cogency of this Colgate analysis. Nothing done in Moscow fulfills or begins to fulfill, the requirements set forth for a world of peace in the atomic era. This being true, we must admit that we are still acting as though we had accepted the first assumption, that there is to be war.

CHAPTER XXII

In the Name of Sanity

I AM SPEAKING in the name of sanity, meaning by sanity the capacity to adjust oneself immediately to reality. To delay a while, to cling to what was reality, but is real no longer, to hope that what is real will pass as a dream, so what has been familiar may be restored, is not sanity. It is mad, somewhat mad or altogether mad.

To living creatures, the real world has always seemed to be expanding. As we developed our senses, its range increased through smell, sight and hearing. As we developed our reason, reality increased even beyond the reach of our senses. The earth, instead of being the flat center of a spangled universe, became a whirling mote in a vast and seething space. As man, too, developed his social qualities, he was able to accumulate knowledge and thereby add to his mastery over matter, and to increase his security. In a swift surge of growth, over the last few thousand years, man has learned to co-operate with other men, as well as to broaden his individual importance. Today we stand at the beginning of the age in which, thanks to world-wide co-operation, combined with the richest of individualism, man has uncovered for his own use the secret of the basic energy of the universe. The long apprenticeship of the human race comes to an end. We have not become gods, but we have wrought for ourselves the tools of creation. I shall not speculate why our first use of these tools should be to make something destructive, something terrible beyond all the terrors that life on this planet has so far encountered. But life is a power to overcome death. We have been disciplined by danger through our entire evolution. In fear we have grown safe. We have had to be nimble and flexible. We have had to develop sanity, the capacity to adjust ourselves immediately to reality.

The challenge to our sanity today is without parallel throughout our existence. The reality of atomic energy is here. Its nature is beyond dispute. We now have the means to destroy masses and civilizations, so that nation no longer can contend against nation, carrying the competition to the battlefield to be decided by the arbitrament of force. Even if men cared to cling to that murderous system, the reality is that the system has gone. In the atomic era anyone who uses atomic destruction to wipe out a foe will bring ruination upon himself and leave only ruin in which to grope to the light again. This being reality, sanity requires our immediate adjustment to it. There must be no more national competitions carried to the battlefield.

The message of atomic energy may at first appear to be only dreadful. But it is the message one might expect when man gains access to the smithy and the anvil of the gods. One might paraphrase it in these words: "You have acquired these powers through social organization and through the integrity of great individuals. You can use them successfully only for the development of organization and individual integrity. And woe be unto you if you seek to use them otherwise, for you will be destroyed."

While it is true that it took a war to produce the final form of the organization which released atomic energy, that release is the first power man has ever had or known strong enough to destroy war. For I am not saying that it is for you and me, and others of fearsome heart, to destroy war. I am saying that the reality is that atomic energy is itself the promise to destroy war, and all human society as well, if we do not adjust ourselves immediately to its reality. It is for us of fearsome heart to hail the end of the long age of national competition. The day of complete co-operation is at hand.

On August 6, 1945, the face of the world was changed. It became clear that America would have to take the leadership of the world in transforming the United Nations into an organization with sufficient power to make and enforce law on an international scale.

Thus we have on our hands a fight even greater than the fight for the United Nations Charter. I do not lay before you a blueprint of a world government as it is to be. But I assert that through the present United Nations Organization there must be developed a world government with limited but adequate powers to prevent war, including power to control the development of atomic energy and other major weapons, and to maintain world inspection and police forces. I believe that the world government should operate through an executive body responsible to a representative legislative assembly; that the legislative assembly should be empowered to enact laws within the scope of the powers conferred upon the world government; that adequate tribunals and enforcement machinery should be established; and finally, that prompt steps should be taken to obtain a constitutional amendment authorizing the United States to join a world government.

It is the inescapable logic of the atomic age that since wars are the acts of sovereign nations, the sovereign power to make war must be ended. For the sovereign nations, in clinging to their right to make war, ordain a condition of anarchy. The only alternative to anarchy is law. There must be law among nations as well as within nations. And there must be the centralized power to enforce law. We can, of course, do nothing, and let war come again. That will end it right enough. Or we can ordain a world of law. One is the way of death. The other is the way of life. One is the way of sanity. The other is the way of suicidal madness.